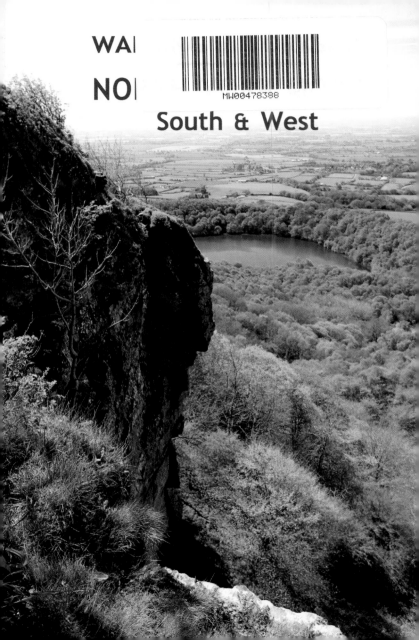

South & West

HILLSIDE GUIDES - ACROSS THE NORTH

Yorkshire River Photobooks •JOURNEY OF THE AIRE
•JOURNEY OF THE WHARFE •JOURNEY OF THE URE

Long Distance Walks
•COAST TO COAST WALK •DALES WAY •CUMBRIA WAY •PENDLE WAY
•WESTMORLAND WAY •FURNESS WAY •CALDERDALE WAY

Circular Walks - North/East Yorkshire
•NORTH YORK MOORS South/West •NORTH YORK MOORS North/East
•HARROGATE & WHARFE VALLEY •HOWARDIAN HILLS

Circular Walks - Yorkshire Dales
•East: NIDDERDALE & RIPON •West: THREE PEAKS & HOWGILL FELLS
•South: WHARFEDALE & MALHAM •North: WENSLEYDALE & SWALEDALE

Circular Walks - Lancashire/North West
•BOWLAND •PENDLE & THE RIBBLE
•LUNESDALE •ARNSIDE & SILVERDALE

Circular Walks - North Pennines
•EDEN VALLEY •ALSTON & ALLENDALE

Circular Walks - South Pennines
•ILKLEY MOOR •BRONTE COUNTRY •CALDERDALE

Hillwalking - Lake District
•LAKELAND FELLS - SOUTH •LAKELAND FELLS - EAST
•LAKELAND FELLS - NORTH •LAKELAND FELLS - WEST

Short Scenic Walks - Yorkshire Dales
•UPPER WHARFEDALE •LOWER WHARFEDALE •INGLETON/WESTERN DALES
•RIBBLESDALE •MALHAMDALE •SWALEDALE •NIDDERDALE
•UPPER WENSLEYDALE •LOWER WENSLEYDALE •SEDBERGH/DENTDALE

Short Scenic Walks - Northern England
•HARROGATE/KNARESBOROUGH •ILKLEY/WASHBURN VALLEY
•AIRE VALLEY •AMBLESIDE/LANGDALE •AROUND PENDLE
•RIBBLE VALLEY •HAWORTH •HEBDEN BRIDGE •BOWLAND

*Send for a detailed current catalogue and price list
and also visit www.hillsidepublications.co.uk*

WALKING in YORKSHIRE

NORTH YORK MOORS
South & West

Paul Hannon

Hillside

HILLSIDE PUBLICATIONS

20 Wheathead Crescent
Keighley
West Yorkshire
BD22 6LX

First published 2015

© Paul Hannon 2015   ISBN 978-1-907626-18-0

Cover illustrations: Urra Moor; Rievaulx Abbey
Back cover: Kilburn White Horse;
Page One: Whitestone Cliff and Gormire Lake
Page Three: On Hawnby Hill; Above: Farndale;
Opposite: Carlton Moor from Whorl Hill
(Paul Hannon/Yorkshire Photo Library)

The sketch maps are based on 1947 Ordnance Survey One-Inch maps

Printed in Malta on behalf of Latitude Press

CONTENTS

INTRODUCTION

The North York Moors National Park covers an area of 553 square miles, and is the best-defined of all the upland areas, rising island-like from the surrounding countryside. This creates an impression of much greater altitude than its modest high point of 1489ft/454m attains. To the north is the Cleveland Plain, westwards the Vales of Mowbray and York, and southwards the Vale of Pickering, while to the east is the ultimate low point, the North Sea. The park itself however has a solid upland mass spreading from the centre towards the western escarpments, where one can walk for mile upon mile and lose little altitude. It is of course all this heather-clad moorland for which the National Park is best known.

Heather moors, despite their profusion, are only one aspect of this diverse region, for here are delightful green valleys and a quite spectacular length of coastline composed largely of rugged cliffs. There are sandy beaches and rocky coves, and inland some shapely summits, fascinating rock outcrops and beautiful waterfalls, while some enchanting indigenous woods remain in addition to large forests. The hand of man has been everywhere, for even the lonely moortops are littered with ancient burial mounds and standing stones. The scores of villages range from fishing ports to moorland farming communities, though many of the villages are to be found beneath the hills, taking advantage of the shelter.

Man has also left ruined abbeys and castles; some old roads including drovers' routes, a Roman road and numerous paved trods; absorbing relics of the former ironstone, alum and jet industries; and not least of all an unrivalled collection of wayside crosses, some being ancient Christian symbols, others serving as waymarks or boundary stones. This is walkers' territory par excellence, with a plethora of long distance and challenge walks crossing it. Best known are the Cleveland Way and the Lyke Wake Walk, while the Coast to Coast Walk ends its classic journey here.

The area is bordered by Scarborough to the south-east, Northallerton to the west and Middlesbrough to the north, while much more closely involved are the fishing port of Whitby and the smaller market towns of Thirsk, Helmsley, Kirkbymoorside, Pickering, Stokesley and Guisborough.

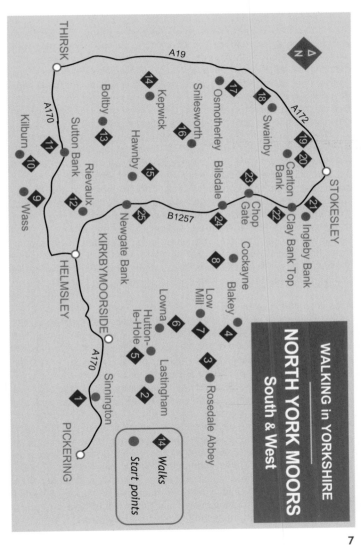

WALKING in YORKSHIRE

NORTH YORK MOORS
South & West

14 Walks

Start points

INTRODUCTION

The two companion titles in this series are divided into well-defined areas that feature much of the best walking. The Southern and Western area includes the bold ridges of the Hambleton Hills and the Cleveland Hills that delineate the western boundary, while a string of south-flowing valleys are divided by high moorland ridges. The parallel rivers of Bilsdale, Bransdale, Farndale and Rosedale squeeze between the Tabular Hills and fuse into the River Rye. Rising in the shadow of the two hill ranges, the Rye's sylvan environs create a perfect foil to the open moors above.

The Hambleton Hills take the form of a broad and undulating whaleback ridge above the Vale of Mowbray, the Cleveland Hills rise rather more aggressively above the Cleveland Plain, while the Tabular Hills rise modestly from the Vale of Pickering to plunge quite sharply at their northern limit into the heart of the Moors. Scattered liberally around the area is a lovely range of villages, from Boltby and Hawnby to Old Byland and Rosedale Abbey. Apart from the beautiful landscapes, further prime attractions include Sutton Bank visitor centre, the Ryedale Folk Museum at Hutton-le-Hole, Beck Isle Museum at Pickering, Helmsley Castle, Rievaulx and Byland Abbeys, Mount Grace Priory near Osmotherley and the 'Mouseman' workshops at Kilburn.

Access to the countryside

The majority of walks are on public rights of way with no access restrictions, or long-established access areas and paths. A handful also take advantage of the 2004 implementation of Right to Roam: any walks making use of Open Country are noted as such in their introduction, though on most days of the year you are free to walk responsibly over these wonderfully invigorating landscapes. Of the restrictions that do pertain, the two most notable are that dogs are normally banned from grouse moors (other than on rights of way); and that the areas can be closed to walkers for up to 28 days each year, subject to advance notice. The most likely times will be from the 'Glorious Twelfth', the start of the grouse shooting season in August, though weekends should largely be unaffected. Further information can be obtained from Natural England, and ideally from information centres. Finally, bear in mind that in spring, avoiding tramping over open country away from paths would help safeguard the crucial period for vulnerable ground-nesting birds.

Using the guide

The walks range from 5 to 8 miles, the average distance being around 6 miles. Each walk is self-contained, essential information being followed by a concise route description and a simple map. Dovetailed in between are snippets of information on features along the way: these are placed in *italics* to ensure the all important route description is easier to locate. Start point postcodes are a rough guide only, for those with 'satnav': grid references are more precise!

The sketch maps serve to identify the location of the routes rather than the fine detail, and whilst the description should be sufficient to guide you around, the appropriate Ordnance Survey map is recommended. To gain the most from a walk, the detail of a 1:25,000 scale Explorer map is unsurpassed. It also gives the option to vary walks as desired, giving a much improved picture of your surroundings and the availability of any linking paths for shortening or lengthening walks. The following map covers all the walks:

• *Explorer OL26 - North York Moors, Western Area*

other than a section of Walk 1 which is found on

• *Explorer OL27 - North York Moors, Eastern Area*

Also useful for planning are Landranger maps 93, 94, 99 and 100.

Useful contacts

North York Moors National Park The Old Vicarage, Bondgate, Helmsley, York YO62 5BP • 01439-772700
Open Access • 0845-100 3298 www.openaccess.naturalengland.org.uk
Information Centres
National Park Centre **Sutton Bank** Thirsk YO7 2EH • 01845-597426
93a Market Place **Thirsk** YO7 1EY • 01845-522755
The Applegarth
Northallerton DL7 8LZ
• 01609-776864
Helmsley Castle
Helmsley YO62 5AB
• 01439-770173
The Ropery
Pickering YO18 8DY
• 01751-473791

Byland Abbey

APPLETON-LE-MOORS

Delightful woodland paths link two super villages by way of the River Seven

START *Sinnington (SE 744857; YO62 6SQ)*

DISTANCE *6¼ miles (10km)*

ORDNANCE SURVEY 1:25,000 MAP
Explorer OL26 - North York Moors West
Explorer OL27 - North York Moors East

ACCESS *Start from the village centre, roadside parking. Scarborough-Helmsley bus.*

Sinnington is a peaceful village of spacious greens by-passed by the main road. All Saints' church boasts some Norman and Saxon work, while a barn opposite was originally a 12th century hall: its east window dates from then, the others three centuries later. For two and a half centuries the village has been the home of the Sinnington Hunt, one of the oldest in the country: a fox graces the maypole outside the old school, while the Fox & Hounds pub also recalls this tradition. Note the defunct little bridge near the graceful central bridge of 1767, and a Methodist chapel of 1795.

Leave the village by the road heading up the east side of the river above the bridge by the green. Passing a fork to the church, the road becomes a track at the last house and drops down to the River Seven at an impressive limestone scar. *Though it is the river of Rosedale, the Seven's finest moments are at Sinnington, where it curves through some exquisitely wooded environs: in springtime these offer fine bluebell displays.* When the river loops away the cart track continues along the bottom of the wood, soon rising a little to a cross-paths on a little brow. Advance straight on, dropping to a gate/stile into an open pasture. With the tree-lined river to the left, a path heads away. As it narrows part way on, rise right to a gate at a break in the wooded bank. Now rise briefly left to a bridle-gate into Hob Bank Wood.

An excellent path now runs a lengthy, generally level course above the river. When a field intervenes, the path is deflected from the river to remain along the bottom of the wood. At a fork towards the end take the main path rising right. Briefly on the edge of the wood, you rapidly reach a junction with a broader way on a small ridge, with a white-walled cottage down to the left. Turn right for a stiff haul through the wood, angling right higher up to rise to a path junction at the top. Turn left for a grand

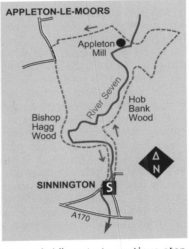

stroll on the wood top, emerging at a bridle-gate to continue atop a bank with open views across the valley.

Towards the end pass through a bridle-gate on the right, and the clear path heads away with a hedge along the top of an unkempt pasture. Through a gate at the end the path bears left then crosses to the far corner of a similar field, where a bridle-gate puts you onto a crossroads of attractive bridleways. Pass through the bridle-gate immediately on your left for a firm, leafy descent to another such gate at the bottom. Drop down to a gate below, from where a tree-lined track drops towards the valley floor. Swinging left at the bottom it runs a broad course between hedgerows to emerge into a field, where it fades. While one bridle-way heads through a gate just ahead, your way is down the widely enclosed path immediately right, rapidly meeting the river again.

Just a few paces downstream cross an arched bridle-bridge over the Seven. *This has replaced a ford at Appleton Mill Farm just downstream, where the old mill and its weir survive.* Turn downstream from the bridge, and a bridle-gate quickly puts you onto the farm access road. Turn right on its hedgerowed course just as far as the start of a wood on the left. Here a cart track heads through a gate on the left into the wood corner. Leave this immediately by a clear path climbing right, an excellent pull through the trees to emerge into the bottom corner of a field. Advance along the tall hedgeside, rising imperceptibly the full length of this narrow field with the roofs of Appleton-le-Moors appearing ahead. At the top corner a stile puts you onto an entirely grassy back lane. Go left just 25 paces to a small gate on the right, and an enclosed path runs between gardens to emerge onto the village street.

Appleton-le-Moors is a classically laid out village with a broad main street. Parallel back lanes run along the rear of both rows of gradely dwellings. The distinguished Christ Church dates from 1865, and a Wesleyan chapel from 1832. The Moors Inn offers refreshment, while the house of three faces is opposite the village hall of 1867, which was originally the school. At the top end, beyond the church, stands the roughly hewn Low Cross, a medieval waymarker showing the route to Lastingham. Turn left along the street, and at the sharp bend at the end keep straight on down a cart track, emerging into a field. *Wide views are now on offer, over the Seven woodlands of your walk to the Wolds beyond the Vale of Pickering, while Sinnington itself soon appears ahead.*

The track makes a pleasant, prolonged descent alongside a hedge: as it levels out towards the bottom, take a bridle-gate at a tiny kink in the hedge. A path crosses newly-planted Fred's Wood to a gate into Bishop Hagg Wood. *Before entering, turn to gaze upon a glorious wooded surround.* A good path resumes high above the river to a bridle-gate back out into a field. Go left along a track to the corner, then keep left along a now enclosed way which closes in on the river. Your way now clings to the tree-lined Seven to lead unerringly back into Sinnington, with the bridge returning you to the main part of the village.

ANA CROSS

A bracing moorland ramble when the heather is in bloom: stout soles are recommended on its stony tracks

START *Lastingham (SE 729904; YO62 6TN)*

DISTANCE *6 miles (9$\frac{1}{2}$km)*

ORDNANCE SURVEY 1:25,000 MAP
Explorer OL26 - North York Moors West

ACCESS *Start from the village centre, roadside parking. Minimal bus from Kirkbymoorside.* •*OPEN ACCESS - see page 8.*

Lastingham is a delightful village that shares an identical situation to its neighbour Hutton-le-Hole, sheltering beneath the wooded Tabular Hills while looking north to the moors. Here the similarity ends. Firstly, Lastingham's houses do not stand quietly back, but huddle round a compact centre with lanes branching off in all directions. The second and more notable difference is that instead of prettiness, Lastingham's pilgrim comes seeking a shrine, that of St Cedd. This Lindisfarne monk founded a monastery in 654, a task completed by his brother Chad. Destroyed by the Danes two centuries later, the site of this important early Christian centre became a place of pilgrimage. In 1078 Stephen of Whitby built a crypt, still intact beneath the present church and a unique Norman relic. Several wells, including one to Cedd, can be found about the village. The Blacksmiths Arms stands in the church's shadow.

From the bridge in the village centre head east away from the church, and at a sharp right turn take the 'no through road' rising left. It climbs out of the village past Lastingham Grange (with refreshments on offer) to lead to a gate onto the open heather moor under Lastingham Knoll, part of the all-embracing Spaunton Moor. *A Millennium stone is supported by a guidepost and a seat at this path crossroads.* Of the departing ways, take the one signed right for Hartoft. This runs briefly alongside the intake wall to soon fork: as the wall swings away right, take the thinner path straight ahead to the right side of a fenced enclosure. Advance along its edge, and at the far end a clear path resumes through returning heather. This quickly reaches a pronounced edge overlooking the broad valley of Tranmire Beck.

The path drops left to the beck, and crosses it immediately beneath a confluence. Of two departing ways, the public footpath rises directly away in a straight line that ascends the moor at a steady gradient to soon arrive at a shooters' track on the broad ridge. Turn left along the track which in the fullness of time will lead unfailingly to Ana Cross. The route thereto is virtually all uphill but only ever gently, some sections being stonier than others. *Passed on the right part way up is a very distinctive hollowed mound identified on the map as an ancient enclosure, with a very modern cairn alongside.*

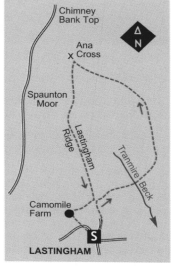

Further, the track swings more up to the left (a lesser one also doubles sharply back right), then beyond a kink continues more to the left. Easing out, another track goes right to a small quarry. Immediately after, Ana Cross appears on the now not-too-distant skyline. A cairn on the right sends a poor track doubling back right as you are now virtually on the brow. A cross-tracks comes before the final rise, to run along to pass just beneath the cross: a thin path runs the 60 strides left to gain it, very much the walk's turning point. *A striking feature on a prominent rise, the 10ft high Ana Cross is a replacement for the original ancient Aine Howe Cross, now found in the church crypt. This is a truly extensive viewpoint, though the broad uplift of moorland rules out valley scenery. To the west and north-east are the rolling moors above Hutton and Rosedale respectively; southwards are the regimented Tabular Hills, and south-east the regimented Cropton Forest.*

From the cross take the broad track heading due south for a very direct return, merging into another such track to maintain the long and very gradual descent of Lastingham Ridge that ultimately takes you back to the moorland furniture beneath Lastingham Knoll: the seat now suggests one last halt. Here you can pleasantly vary the finish by ignoring the gate to claim one last stretch of moorland. Turn right with the wall to find a little path dropping down the side through heather to cross a small stream, then a short pull up the other side to run on to a wall corner above Camomile Farm. Turn left here to find a corner gate left of the buildings. From it follow the short access road down open ground to emerge onto the road at the western end of the village.

Lastingham

HEART OF ROSEDALE

A magnificent high-level stroll on the old ironstone railway sandwiched between a steep climb and a valley return

START *Rosedale Abbey (SE 724959; YO18 8RT)*

DISTANCE *5 miles (8km)*

ORDNANCE SURVEY 1:25,000 MAP
Explorer OL26 - North York Moors West

ACCESS *Start from the village centre, car park.*

Rosedale Abbey is a lovely village in the true heart of the National Park. It is also a busy little place, with pubs, cafes, shop and caravan sites. Its name stems from the existence of a Cistercian nunnery founded here in the mid-12th century. What little remains stands forlornly in a small enclosure behind the church of St Mary & St Laurence (1839), and is seen at the end of the walk. Much of the remains were plundered for dwellings during the 19th century ironstone boom (see also WALK 4). Roads radiate from strategically sited Rosedale Abbey, including two which cross the high moors to a range of Eskdale villages.

Leave the village centre by the 'Hutton-le-Hole via Chimney Bank' road, which runs alongside a stream before quickly bridging it. Leave immediately by a small gate ahead, right of a house, and up steps to a stile into a field. A steep ascent up the side leads to a stile onto another road. From a stile opposite, rise past a golf clubhouse, and on the course immediately slant right across it to locate a ladder-stile in a wall. A path ascends rough pasture to another such stile at the top, onto the foot of the open moor. This now rises left through bracken above the golf course wall, then swings more uphill to ease out with a fence returning on the left.

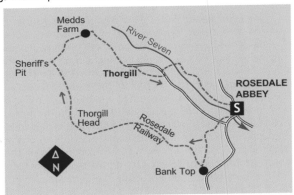

Rising to a stile in an intervening fence you enter heather moor, and the path curves up to the right, still shadowed by a fence on the left. A much easier rise leads up, ascending towards the houses of Bank Top. *These are all that survive from a railway workers' community, while further left you can see the kilns of the former ironstone mine. A tall chimney also stood here until its demolition in 1972.* The wispish path bears right of the houses, merging with a broader green way rising to some remains, with a hard track just behind. This rises right just a few strides to merge into the old railway. *The railway arrived in 1861 in order to efficiently remove the increasing amounts of ironstone being mined in the valley, a job initially undertaken by horses: see also WALK 4.*

Turn right to commence the easiest of walking, almost 1$\frac{3}{4}$ miles along its splendid course high above the valley with commensurate views. Passing a bench, it soon swings left in a big arc around the little side valley of Thorgill. Beyond Thorgill Head it swings back out to quickly arrive at Sheriff's Pit. *The scant remains of the mine manager's house are the frail survivor of numerous buildings. Ironstone mining took place here for around half a century from*

1857 until 1911, its heyday being the 1870s. Also surviving is a fenced shaft some 270ft deep and still with the sound of running water. From here are views across the deep valley to the mighty kilns at Rosedale East Mines, visited in WALK 4.

At this point you depart back to the valley, guided by a low waymark sending two paths down the moor. Yours is the left option, signed for Medds Farm. This descends pleasantly, before long arriving at a reedy, sunken section. A waymark points you slightly right of the main groove, dropping more markedly alongside low crags with isolated rowans decorating a channel on your left. *From here a horizontal tunnel struck some 1500ft through the hillside to connect with the bottom of the mineshaft just visited.*

The path then drops down again to a gate off the moor. It then continues down a bracken pasture with a wall on the left, easing out to run all the way to its tapering end at the rear of Medds Farm. Pass through a small gate into the confines, with an old barn on your right and a cottage on the left. *Pit ponies from the mine above were stabled here.* Take a gate on the right to pass along the front of the main house, and out along the driveway. Very quickly branch left down a little enclosed path to join an access road. Turn right on this to merge with the drive you've just left, and through a gate head off along the valley to shortly arrive at Thorgill, a good Norse name if ever there was.

Rosedale from under Bank Top *Opposite: Thorgill Head*

Head through the hamlet and leave the road as it swings sharp left on a little brow after crossing a bridge below the phonebox. Don't take the cart track doubling back right from this grassy patch, instead take an enclosed path rising directly from the junction. A kissing-gate puts you in a field, where head away with the wall on your left. A briefly enclosed spell encounters some sections of old causey and a stone trough, emerging to resume to another kissing-gate at the end. Transferring to the wall's other side continue along a field top, and from a gate at the end head down the field centre to a gate opposite, with another onto the road just behind it.

Go left just 100 paces and from a bridle-gate on the right, a path crosses a field to a footbridge on the tree-lined infant River Seven. Rise a few paces to a path junction and go right to a bridle-gate out of the trees. The path runs briefly beneath a wooded bank before slanting across the grassy bank, to then run on above trees to a gate/stile. It runs on further above the trees before slanting gently down to a kissing-gate at the far corner onto a caravan site access road. *Alongside the drive is Waterhouse Well, which once provided water for the priory. The intriguing shelter around it is complete with an internal stone seat.* Head along the track, past a recreation area then turning off left on a short green way to a wall-stile onto the road. Emerging opposite the nunnery remains at the back of the church, turn right along the back road to the green.

ROSEDALE RAILWAY

A supremely easy walk around a fascinating valley head from the perfect platform of a Victorian mineral railway

START *Blakey (SE 683989; YO62 7LQ)*

DISTANCE *8 miles (12³4km)*

ORDNANCE SURVEY 1:25,000 MAP
Explorer OL26 - North York Moors West

ACCESS *Start from a moorland car park on the Hutton-le-Hole-Castleton road, at the Farndale junction half a mile south of the Lion Inn. Seasonal Moorsbus. •OPEN ACCESS - see page 8.*

From the car park you immediately look down on the head of Rosedale to the east, and a footpath sign points the way less than 100 strides to meet the old railway. *The Rosedale Ironstone Railway was constructed in 1861 to carry iron ore from the Rosedale mines to the furnaces on Teesside. One cannot fail to be impressed by this achievement of engineering: running across the moors over 1000 feet up, the line climbed from the valley by way of a steep incline (see WALK 21) then contoured around the head of Farndale to Blakey, where your walk begins. The car park stands on Blakey Ridge's narrowest point, and a junction developed here in 1865 when the line to the mines on the west side of Rosedale was joined by the line you shall return on, round the dalehead serving the East Mines. The railway closed in 1929 with the demise of mining, but both have left their mark. Today it is difficult to visualise a scene of thousands toiling in this now tranquil dale.*

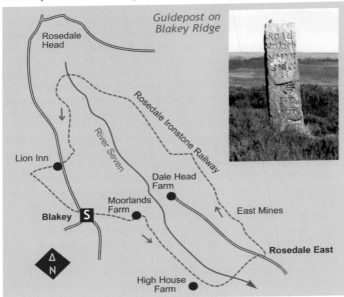

Guidepost on Blakey Ridge

Rosedale Head

Rosedale Ironstone Railway

River Seven

Lion Inn

Dale Head Farm

Moorlands Farm

Blakey S

East Mines

Rosedale East

N

High House Farm

At the outset, virtually the entire route can be surveyed. For now go only a stride or two to the right to an information panel, and then head down the slope on an inviting grassy path. Lower down it meets a wide track which takes you more gently down to Moorlands Farm. Enter the yard and bear right down the surfaced access road dropping away. Quickly leave this by a bridleway that heads off through a gate on the right. This runs unfailingly as a fine grassy track (Daleside Road) through countless fields, sometimes enclosed. Its generally excellent course becomes firmer before joining a driveway at a renovated farm with a fine range of out-buildings. Continue along this firmer access road until less than a hundred paces after the next access road comes down from High House Farm up to the right. Here take a stile on the left and descend the field to a footbridge on the infant River Seven.

A path slants left up the bank, then from a gate ascend with a fence on the left up two fieldsides to Craven Garth Farm. Continue up past holiday cottages to emerge onto the road serving Rosedale East. Go briefly right to a brow just ahead. *En route you pass the Orange Tree relaxation centre, which was until relatively recently an absorbing Post office/store, one of the last of its breed: the only clue today is a Victorian postbox in its wall. The Ebenezer Methodist Chapel of 1872 more recently incorporated the Rosedale Centre, but in 2014 was on the market. This little community is a surprising place to find this far up the valley, its existence being due to the ironstone mining era: the terrace of Hill Cottages housed miners, and others survive nearby.*

Here turn sharp left up a rough access road passing a lone house. *Behind it are the three compartments of former coal bunkers from the station above.* Reaching a gate just above, the bridleway turns right, but you advance straight ahead past a barn and farming detritus. *This is the site of the old goods station.* After the fenced ruin on the left bear left a few strides to alight onto the grassy course of the old railway itself. Turn right, and this time you are to become well acquainted - all the way back to Blakey, in fact. However when you get striding out don't think you've cracked it, there's still a good 4$\frac{1}{2}$ miles back to Blakey Junction!

Various features of the East Mines are rapidly encountered. Almost at once you pass the 16 compartments of the calcining kilns, while up behind is a ventilation chimney and a forlorn entrance arch to an adit. A little further along are the three 'iron' kilns, still enormous but more ruinous. Buildings up behind are Black Houses (miners' cottages) alongside workshops. Looking across the valley, it might be noticed that your start point is appreciably higher than the East Mines, so clearly the old railway had to make a gradual descent around the dalehead from Blakey.

Beyond the mines the line runs on to a sizeable embankment with woodland on its far side, where a track drops away to Dale Head Farm tea garden. Then comes the mighty heather-clad Reeking Gill embankment, with a colourful ravine upstream featuring an iron-rich spring. Immediately off it the path surmounts the left-hand spur as the railway enters a reed-choked cutting. A good moorland path remains alongside the reedy channel all the way to a major turning point at the dalehead embankment on the tiny Seven.

The old way swings back out to now head down-dale, with new views to match. One further reedy interruption occurs before normal service resumes on what is a very discernible pull to the red-brick remains of a water tower. A little beyond a pool on your left, a signed path branches right. *Whilst the easiest option is to remain on the track to quickly reach the starting point, an easy variation finish takes in the Lion Inn and a look into Farndale.* Take the inviting path slanting up the moor towards Blakey House, deflected by its fence up onto the road where the Lion awaits! *The Lion Inn dates back over 400 years: once thriving with iron and coal miners, today it refreshes countless walkers and tourists.*

Your onward route is straight across to Blakey Howe behind the pub. *The standing stone on this ancient burial mound enjoys views of both Rosedale and Farndale.* Go briefly right to the wall corner behind it, meeting another path to go left down the wallside: when the wall ends continue down the short way to rejoin the railway – now around the head of Farndale. Turn left for a very different view of a different valley from the same route as you've just left in Rosedale. This leads quickly and unfailingly back to Blakey Junction. *On arrival you are greeted by the blocked former tunnel.*

Kilns at Rosedale East Mines

23

GILLAMOOR

*Mostly easy walking linking two villages high above the
River Dove via open common, rich woodland and old mills*

START *Hutton-le-Hole (SE 704901; YO62 6UA)*

DISTANCE *6^{1}2 miles (10^{1}2km)*

ORDNANCE SURVEY 1:25,000 MAP
Explorer OL26 - North York Moors West

ACCESS *Start from the village centre, car park.
Seasonal Sunday and twice weekly bus service.*

Hutton-le-Hole is probably the best-known inland village in
the National Park, and in summer its popularity is all too evident.
Its charms are open to view, with its beck, bridges and ubiquitous
sheep tending its extensive greens. The Crown Inn and several tearooms offer refreshment. Things to look for include the old cattle
pound and tiny St Chad's church with the Mouseman's work.
Hutton's position is also superb, sheltering under the Tabular Hills
with moors rising to the north. Aside from its obvious assets,
Hutton's special feature is the Ryedale Folk Museum. Its excellent
presentation of local life in bygone days is crowned by a first-class
range of reconstructed moor dwellings.

From the village centre take the Castleton road, and leave by
a gate on the left where the parallel side road comes in (after the
last house on the left). Go right with the hedge to a corner kissing-

gate, then bear left to another such gate onto a hedgerowed path. Turn left along this leafy way to its demise, then continue along a cornfield side to emerge via a kissing-gate onto bracken-cloaked common. *Ahead is a grand expanse of moorland, Harland Moor and beyond, and a range of Tabular Hills to the left.* Go left a few paces to a path coming out from the adjacent gate: almost at once this meets a broader green way. Go left, but at an early fork take the better one bearing right across the common. Within fifty paces, however, take a slimmer, grassy path right through bracken to descend slowly, aiming for red-roofed Grouse Hall.

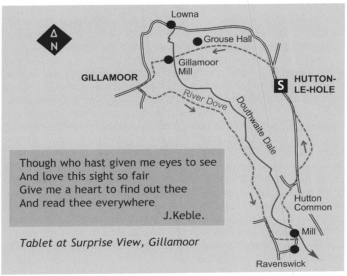

> Though who hast given me eyes to see
> And love this sight so fair
> Give me a heart to find out thee
> And read thee everywhere
>
> J.Keble.

Tablet at Surprise View, Gillamoor

Soon after crossing the drain of an old water-cut, another such way merges from the right. Bearing left this narrows to drop towards a fence corner, and the path angles down before it to drop onto a cart track. Go left just a few strides then drop down to a footbridge into a field. Cross straight over beneath the farm to a stile, and across again to one in the next field corner. A hedge is then followed left down to a corner gate, and down a smaller field to a wooden footbridge across the River Dove.

25

From the bridge advance towards Gillamoor Mill, but in front of the nearest building bear right on a grass track around to a gate, and on again to the far end of the attractive grouping of buildings. From a gate a green way rises to merge into the steeply-climbing access road. Above a sharp bend right it levels out: at this point double back left into trees on a path that contours briefly before commencing a sustained slant beneath a steep, wooded bank. This excellent way rises up to emerge suddenly by way of old quarries onto a green alongside the church at Gillamoor. *This street village on the edge of a plateau is renowned for its Surprise View: here Farndale, Lowna and Blakey Ridge feature in a glorious vista from just north of St Aidan's church. Note also a Wesleyan Methodist Memorial Chapel of 1867 complete with a working 'Farndale' clock, and the Royal Oak pub further along the street.*

Head along the street and left at the junction by the pub and school, then leave the road at the first bend by taking the narrow lane straight ahead. After just a few minutes, beyond sports fields take a gate on the left and head directly away along a hedgeside. At a gate at the end the way becomes briefly enclosed: at the end take the left-hand gate to resume along another hedgeside, now on your right. At the end drop to a corner gate from where a track slants down through a wood. Emerging at a gate, the fainter track runs pleasantly across a sheep pasture with open views, re-entering woodland at the other side. Soon leaving the trees again, this time a longer open spell is enjoyed on a good grassy track for a sustained length between river and forest in Douthwaite Dale. *This southern continuation of Farndale relates to the short length of the valley where the Dove breaks through the Tabular Hills to leave the moors.*

Finally re-entering the woods again, an angled cross-tracks awaits just ahead, where the bridleway bears along the broad track to the left. It is left just after the trees on the left end at a gate into open pasture, where your route is a thinner, well-sunken way slanting up to the right. This rises to a level green track at mid-height. Go left a few strides then resume your climb up a broad track to reach a fork as you finally level out. Go right to quickly join a harder forest road, and turn left between woods and crop fields. After about half a mile you emerge onto the sharp bend of a surfaced road: go left for a few minutes. Immediately beyond an old timber yard, a footpath sign sends a tightly enclosed path down into some undergrowth. This soon opens out in woodland, meeting a rough track. Resume left down this, quickly meeting another on a bend, and bearing right down it onto a road below Ravenswick.

Turn left to the road-end alongside a solitary, red-brick former mill, and just a little beyond the adjacent ford is a footbridge over the Dove. Passing another house, follow a rough road climbing steeply away to the open country of Hutton Common, easing to meet the Douthwaite Dale farm road. *Extensive views open out over the dale, to Harland Moor and beyond.* With the Hutton-le-Hole to Kirkbymoorside road in view ahead, a thin path takes a brief short-cut left across the common. Joining the road go left over the cattle-grid and past a parking area. *For a straightforward finish simply remain on the road to drop down into the village.*

A more varied conclusion leaves the road just as it starts to drop away at a lay-by. Cross to a gate set back on the right, from where a path heads away left between patches of scrub. Within just a few strides however, veer left through a gap from where a broader path slants down a wooded bank, narrowing to arrive at a footbridge on Hutton Beck. Cross to the right of the trees opposite for a steep little pull up a sheep pasture, bearing left towards the top to a stile ahead. A thin, tortuous fifty strides through nettles leads to emerge onto an access road, only avoided by mistakenly veering further left to a gate onto the access road. Turn left over a cattle-grid and remain on this road which drops down then runs pleasantly on to arrive back in the village.

Hutton-le-Hole

27

HARLAND MOOR

A super mix of woodland and moorland in 'hidden' Farndale

START *Lowna (SE 685910; YO62 7JU)*

DISTANCE *5¹⁄₄ miles (8¹⁄₂km)*

ORDNANCE SURVEY 1:25,000 MAP
Explorer OL26 - North York Moors West

ACCESS *Start from a small car park west of Lowna Farm beneath the Farndale turning on the Gillamoor to Hutton-le-Hole road.*

Lowna is nothing more than a farmstead, but from the road down to the bridge the prominent large old building was once a tannery. This is a delightful setting by the River Dove, with the steep Gillamoor Bank rising to that village less than a mile distant. From the car park don't return to the road, but instead take the track leaving the rear of the parking area. It soon narrows to drop down to cross a small stream (footbridge/ford), turning downstream a few strides to a guidepost and fork. Take the left one which soon passes beneath an old burial ground of the Society of Friends. *Easily missed is this small walled enclosure at the bottom corner of a wood. A notice by the gate records the fact that between the years 1675 and 1837, 114 Quakers were buried here.*

The path now rises gently through bracken alongside a wall across the bottom of Harland Moor. *Harland Moor is a fine area of moorland divided by the Gillamoor-Low Mill road: colourful* bracken slopes, interspersed with rowan, descend almost to the river. A kissing-gate at the end puts you into a plantation, and the path drops down to a junction above the River Dove. Turn upstream on the upper path which keeps well above the river's immediate environs, through claustrophobically dense bracken in late summer but remaining a good path underneath. Through a long, broad clearing beneath telegraph poles, the path gradually narrows to delve into silver birch and drop down towards the river at the end, soon arriving at Dale End footbridge on the Dove.

Fresh from escaping all the excitement of its daffodil crowds around Low Mill, the River Dove now settles down to flow through some exquisitely wooded and very peaceful environs. And shunning any further publicity it glides out of the park to join the River Rye in the flat Vale of Pickering. Don't

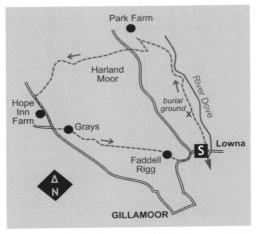

cross the river but take the path climbing steeply left: it soon eases to swing right, rising near the wall enclosing the wood and up onto a broad green way. Ignore a stile in front and turn right on this level course. When the way swings left and gently uphill away from the wall (at a small kink in it), the true path advances straight on a slender wallside way.

Through denser bracken it reaches a cart track ascending from a gate in the wall, which climbs left to a gate in the top corner. *Great views look up Farndale at this point, and will soon further improve.* It then slants up beneath a scattering of trees to meet the driveway to isolated Park Farm. Don't enter but turn left along this to quickly reach a gate onto the open country of Harland Moor.

Advance along this drive for a further 150 or so paces, then locate a slender path doubling back up to the right at a small cairn. Once found it is completely clear as it enjoys a glorious slant up the moor through heather and bilberry bushes, with fine views up into the heart of Farndale. It quickly runs above a wall-corner and over a grass track to emerge onto a moorland road.

Cross straight over and along a good Landrover track through the heather of Harland Moor. A gentle rise precedes a lengthy level section, before descending gradually as it narrows to a footpath. Eventually leaving the moor at a gate/stile, a short way along the wallside a gate on the left precedes a footbridge over Harland Beck. *The adjacent ford is usually sufficient for the crossing, and indeed is worth using in order not to miss the remarkable spring just a couple of steps upstream. Here, right at your feet, is the answer to the red beck, for the spring, within a stride of the stream on the bank, spills forth a gaudy hue of iron-coloured water into the previously clear stream, quite impressive!*

A track doubles back up left to a wall with a wall corner just ahead, and a continuing path crosses rougher moorland by an old wall to a converging wall corner. Here it bears left across further rough pasture to a gate between wall and fence. From it take the slender but clear path through the heather, diagonally across a curious little moor to a densely wooded corner preceding a bridle-gate onto a road.

Turn left along the road past the brow at Hope Inn Farm to soon drop down to a minor junction. Just a few steps further take a stile on the left and cross a small enclosure where a track leads the short way into the yard at Grays Farm. *This farmstead has the traditional appearance of the Danish-style long house, with less traditional solar panels covering its red pantiles.* Cross to a gate opposite and across a field to another gate/stile. Across a further field a bridle-gate puts you onto the right-angle of a bridleway: advance straight on an increasingly enclosed way. Initially rather overgrown, it quickly improves into a cart track. Entering a wood corner keep straight on the main way, and quickly reaching the end, again keep straight on the hard track to run between hedgerows to the attractively arranged Faddell Rigg Farm. Again keep straight ahead on the access road dropping down onto a road. Turn left to soon return to the car park just beyond the Farndale junction.

FARNDALE

An enthralling contrast between the daffodil river in the valley bottom and hugely colourful wilder country above

START *Low Mill (SE 672952; YO62 7JZ)*

DISTANCE *6$\frac{1}{2}$ miles (10$\frac{1}{2}$km)*

ORDNANCE SURVEY 1:25,000 MAP
Explorer OL26 - North York Moors West

ACCESS *Start from the village centre, small car park.*

Farndale is renowned for its springtime carpet of daffodils, the result being a temporary one-way road system and little chance to wander lonely as a cloud. Don't be put off by this - any crowds will soon be left behind. The reason for this profusion of yellow has been attributed to the monks of Rievaulx and also to Nicholas Postgate, 'martyr of the moors', who dubbed them 'lenten lilies'. Designation of Farndale Nature Reserve in 1953 was almost insufficient to avoid a threatened massive 1960s reservoir a little up-dale: hard to believe that so recently people were still so blind. Opposite the car park is an idyllic picture postcard scene featuring what until 2006 was the Post office, while the village hall and WCs also stand by the car park.

From the car park entrance take the adjacent gate to a foot-bridge over the River Dove. The footpath now follows the Dove upstream, and as this forms the 'daffodil walk' there is little chance

31

of going astray. *Note how the meandering Dove covers twice the ground you do! Good views look right up to Blakey Ridge.* Various gates are encountered on this path that is solid underfoot all the way to arrival at High Mill. *The seasonal Daffy Caffy sits amid this attractive cluster.* From here a narrow lane takes you away from the river to Church Houses. *While here a worthwhile visit (besides the Feversham Arms) is to St Mary's church, hidden in trees two minutes up the road to Low Mill. Rebuilt in 1871, a community of friars existed here in the Middle Ages. Church Houses is also the setting for the annual Farndale Show each August.*

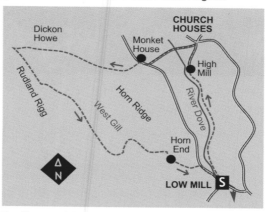

At the first road junction turn left to drop down to re-cross the Dove on a stone-arched bridge before a steep climb to a junction. *You have already earned a grand view across the dale, with Blakey Ridge on the skyline and steep Blakey Bank descending to Church Houses and the patchwork fields of the valley.* Turn briefly right as far as Monket House, where from a gate on the left a rutted track climbs the rough pasture to a gate onto the open moor. Passing old quarries it slants further over Monket House Bank, and ignoring two lesser branches it eases out to stride through luxuriant heather. *Massive views look right to the dalehead, its skyline is formed by the Rosedale ironstone railway.* Only negligibly gaining height, you ultimately reach a crossroads with the Rudland Rigg 'road'. *This rough old road is a splendid walkers' highway, once a major route*

between communities north and south of the moorland barrier. Turn left for a little under half a mile, on a very gentle descent along the broad ridge. *Views are largely confined to the parallel ridges of Bilsdale Moors to the right and Blakey Ridge to the left.*

Passing a bridleway waymark in the slight dip, rise little more than a hundred paces further to a crossroads with a grassy track. Here leave the ridge and turn left on this inviting broad path going steadily down past a string of grouse butts. Towards the end of these the now narrower path passes between butts to run a largely level course right through bracken and heather. *Between West Gill and the main valley, the clean-cut profile of Horn Ridge dominates the secluded, richly-coloured side valley.* Before long the path arrives at the edge of a more pronounced minor drop, marked by a cairn. Don't descend the stony little way with a wall corner just down to the left, but remain on your super path continuing along the level brow, aiming for a solitary rowan tree. A little beyond it you round the head of a dry ravine and slant down a little through the bracken, but soon returning to begin a prolonged, delightful contour with the steeper edge of Double Crag set back to the right.

Further, faced with a hummocky slope in front, the path winds down to the left to a gate in the intake wall just below. From it a green path heads away, but leave the continuing one for a near immediate left fork, dropping down past a modest spoil heap to cross to a gate in the descending wall just to the left. Rather more faintly it loops away from the wall to curve down to a wooden bridge on West Gill Beck. Across, double back right to a gate out into a pasture, and slant away from the beck to a corner gate/stile. A nice grassy cart track heads on past High Barn to run on to Horn End Farm. Alongside the buildings continue away on its access road to drop down to a road, with Low Mill now just five minutes along to the right.

Old sign at Low Mill

WALK 8

BRANSDALE

*Excellent walking on good paths and tracks
in and above a secret valley*

START *Cockayne (SE 620983; YO62 7JL)*

DISTANCE *6$\frac{1}{4}$ miles (10km)*

ORDNANCE SURVEY 1:25,000 MAP
Explorer OL26 - North York Moors West

ACCESS *Start from a road junction just beneath the church,
roadside parking by cattle-grid. •OPEN ACCESS - see page 8.*

Some 10 miles from Helmsley and Kirkbymoorside, the hamlet
of Cockayne is Bransdale's largest settlement. Alongside Bransdale
Lodge is the tiny church of St Nicholas, an isolated gem erected in
1886 on a much older site. Bransdale is a 'hidden' valley, a great
upland bowl that narrows at its 'foot' as Hodge Beck makes its
escape to begin a new life at Kirkdale. From the cattle-grid take the
Kirkbymoorside road down across the beck. The road climbs away,
and after the second sharp bend right, take a gate/stile on the left.
A little path shadows a sunken way up the wallside to a gate at the
top onto open moorland. A grassy way rises right near the wall,
then swings left to the top corner of the plantation. It runs left
above the trees, but within 30 paces bears off right, rising across
the heather moor. This soon eases and swings right to meet a
shooters' track. *For a short-cut go right to the Rudland Rigg 'road'.*

The main route goes left, running along to meet the Rudland Rigg 'road'. Just before it, 35 paces down to the left is the old guidepost of Cockam (Cockayne) Cross. *Most prominent of its inscriptions are 'Bransdale Rode' and 'Farndale Rd', though it also features the main objectives of the rigg road as 'Stoxi (Stokesley) Rode' and 'Kirby (Kirkbymoorside) Rode'. The upper section of the shaft stands in the base, with the lower half recumbent alongside. The rough road along Rudland Rigg is an ancient highway which runs a magnificent ridge-top course linking villages to north and south of the high moors.*

Double back right along the splendid track for about 1½ miles as far as a crossroads with a track of equal stature. *During this march enjoy views left to Farndale and right into Bransdale, the walk's highest point of 1341ft/409m coming almost at once. As the short-cut track comes in, across to the right are the prominent Bronze Age burial cairns of the Three Howes. Before the crossroads, another old stone inscribed 'Kirby Rode' is passed.*

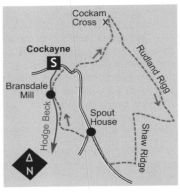

Dropping gently to the crossroads of old ways turn right, over the reedy headwaters of Ouse Gill and up to a gentle brow. Fork left here on a shooters' track that drops gently along the broad crest of Shaw Ridge. After a long half-mile it makes a briefly more marked descent past a prominent cairn. On levelling out, turn right on a thin path which makes a very steady descent through heather to meet a road. *If the path is missed, the track joins the same road further on.* Go right, descending with some glorious Bransdale views to a cattle-grid off the moor and down to a minor junction at Spout House Farm. *Note the line of stone troughs in front of the fine range of outbuildings.*

Go left past the farm, then take a gate/stile on the right and descend a wallside. Towards the bottom is a gate onto the other side, and then down a short way with a tiny stream to another gate. Now bear right along a field top, bridging the stream at the end. Through a gate, cross to another opposite and head away with the wall on your left. As the wall turns off, slant down to the far corner overlooking Hodge Beck. Ignore the wall-stile on your left and drop right to a stone-slab crossing of a sidestream. Two paths head away from the bridle-gate behind: take the left one over a slight brow and along the bank top high above the beck. At a wood corner at the end, keep on above the trees to a small gate. Advance on again over an open bank to drop to twin bridle-gates flanking a sidestream. Cross the field to another sidestream and gate into the tree-lined environs of the beck. A super little part-flagged path runs in its company to quickly reach Bransdale Mill.

This splendid group of buildings is based on an 18th century cornmill, partly rebuilt in 1842 by William Strickland. Working into the 1950s, it has seen some restoration by the National Trust as an outdoor base. Some easily missed features include a free-standing sundial in the field up to the left, and an intriguing inscription on the side porch as you leave. Resume on the access track right of the mill, on above the beck then rising right, up and around a field-side to meet the road on which you began. Turn left to finish.

St Nicholas' church, Cockayne

BYLAND ABBEY

A delight all the way, saving the highlight for the end

START *Wass (SE 554793; YO61 4BE)*

DISTANCE *5³4 miles (9¹4km)*

ORDNANCE SURVEY 1:25,000 MAP
Explorer OL26 - North York Moors West

ACCESS *Start from the village centre. Limited roadside parking, village hall car park with honesty box just past church.*

Wass is a small village sheltered beneath the wooded Hambleton Hills. Set around a crossroads, central feature is the Wombwell Arms. Up the side road to Wass Bank is the tiny St Thomas's church, complete with a clock and bell outside. Head up the 'no through road' from the crossroads opposite the pub. This quickly becomes a rough lane as it rises into a wood. At the end is a fork as the access road swings right for Lund Farm. Use neither track but go straight ahead to a kissing-gate into a field. Head away outside the bluebell wood, a grand little path passing beneath a bright gorse bank. Further along it bears right into a woodland corner. Merging with another path from the right it rises gently through scattered trees, and quickly along to a stile into denser woodland.

The wood is entered at a hairpin bend on a forest track. Take the level left branch, which drops briefly then climbs steeply to a junction as it levels out. Take a waymarked path straight ahead,

37

ascending the wooded bank then slanting right to a brow: here the going eases and the path runs along the well-defined crest of a wooded ridge. After the ridge broadens, the path drops onto a forest track just as it rises from the left to level out at a clearing. Bear right along this green way through open woodland to the wood edge. From a stile in front follow a wallside along the length of two cornfields. Emerging into a sheep pasture at the end, Cam Farm appears ahead. Bear left near the fence and cross to the far side of the farm, and from a gate head past the barn to a gate ahead.

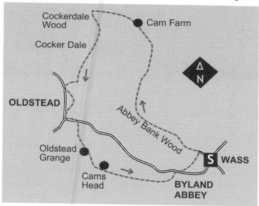

Now bear left to pass along the outside of the garden wall at Cam House. *Big views look left over the Cocker Dale woodland and out to the plains.* Keep straight on through a few trees to a gate just ahead, through which a splendid green track descends into Cockerdale Wood. Dropping down to pass through a gate, it levels out and runs along to meet a rougher forest road. Double back left on this, dropping sharply right and on to a fork at a stream crossing. Turn left over the tiny stream and away along the forest road through Great Cockerdale Wood, amid much tree felling. This leads on and down to the edge of the wood, re-crossing the stream on a broad bridge to leave the wood at a junction of ways. Keep left on the main way, becoming fully surfaced and running pleasantly along to meet another lane from the right. Keep left to quickly arrive at a T-junction with the Kilburn-Oldstead back road.

Turning left, either remain on the road or use this more varied entry into the village: turn left almost at once along the next drive to Oldstead Hall, but approaching the houses take a waymarked path on the right. This zigzags up the steep bank and over a stile, then left along a bluebell bank above the wood. At the top corner of the wood continue up to a bridle-gate. A brief enclosed section along the wood top emerges at another bridle-gate. Turn sharp right to follow the hedge towards the houses. A garden corner deflects you left to a gate onto a short drive out onto the road.

Oldstead is a typical small sub-Hambleton village of scattered cottages. Go left to a junction by the Black Swan. Bear left a short way and within a hundred strides of passing the village sign take the first drive right. This leads through fields to Oldstead Grange. Pass through the yard between barns and house, and at the barns' end slant down the field on a grassy track to bridge a tiny stream. Across, bear sharp left on a path rising through trees and up to emerge at the field corner. Go right to an outer fence corner then left to a stile in the very corner. The way now heads along a tall, lengthy hedgeside, with the house at Cams Head to the left.

At a corner gate/stile transfer to the other side. *Over to the left the southernmost Hambleton Hills are draped in dense, mainly natural woodland, while from the stile look further back left for a nice cameo of Kilburn's White Horse.* Two fields further, abandon the tiny stream and rise slightly to a kissing-gate beneath a lone tree. Continue on through monastic earthworks to join a hedge on the left, and with Byland Abbey just ahead, follow this along to emerge via a stile onto a road. Turn left to Byland Abbey.

Byland Abbey comprises of the abbey itself, the salubrious Abbey Inn and tearoom, and odd dwellings. Over the side road past the inn is a 13th century gatehouse. In the care of English Heritage, this lovely Cistercian site is dominated by the tall West front high above extensive low-level remains. The founding of the abbey is quite a story, as the monks constantly moved sites until settling here in 1177. The abbey was dissolved in 1538. Continue along the Wass road just beyond the junction, and take the first drive on the left to Abbey House. Leave at once by a stile on the right and cross to another into a larger pasture. Head left up the bank to the far corner to find a seat and a kissing-gate. Cross to another gate and straight on to a final one onto the lane on which the walk began.

THE WHITE HORSE

*A classic walk along the Hambleton escarpment
with an array of fascinating features*

START *Kilburn (SE 513796; YO61 4AH)*

DISTANCE *6$\frac{1}{2}$ miles (10$\frac{1}{2}$km)*

ORDNANCE SURVEY 1:25,000 MAP
Explorer OL26 - North York Moors West

ACCESS *Start from the village centre, roadside parking.
Alternative starts: White Horse car park near top of White
Horse Bank; White Horse Bank car park near foot of bank.*

    *Kilburn is the home of two famous Yorkshire 'pets'. Aside from
its White Horse of which more shortly, at the hub of the village
are the workshops begun by Robert Thompson, the 'Mouseman',
where the little carved mouse climbs his furniture. This delightful
trademark can be found in numerous churches, pubs and houses in
and beyond the county. It is open to visitors and features a café.
The village itself is also highly attractive, with a tiny stream
running by well-maintained cottages and gardens. In the square
are the Forresters Arms, a war memorial and an old mounting
block. St Mary's church boasts a solid 15th century tower.*
    *From the square head north through the village, keeping
straight on the main road with some decent verges for a long half-
mile to a junction at the foot of White Horse Bank. En route, the*

White Horse looms dramatically ahead. At once the left fork begins to climb, soon entering trees. Just above White Horse Bank car park a path goes off right, climbing through the trees parallel with the road for a considerable time. On drawing level with the main White Horse car park, take a gap in the adjacent fence to cross the road into it. With the horse now directly above, take the steep, stepped path up the side of it to level out at the top.

The White Horse of Kilburn is a landmark of Yorkshire pride, though many have only observed it from afar: the 19-mile distant tower of York Minster is a popular vantage point for the sharp-eyed. This amazing creature was the brainchild of businessman Thomas Taylor: over 300 feet long, it was carved out of the hillside by the village schoolmaster in 1857. What sets this apart from its southern cousins is the fact that its base is not of chalk, and consequently requires regular up-keep: visitors are begged not to walk on it. Its

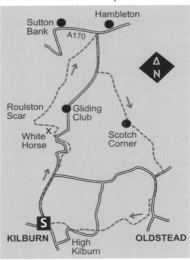

very size means it is more satisfactorily appraised from the vicinity of the village than when you're actually up here! The views out, however, are far-reaching, looking south over the gently rolling Howardian Hills to the more distant line of the Yorkshire Wolds.

The path runs left above the top of the horse, the best view-point for it being at the far end. On leaving, the firm path resumes left to rapidly emerge above Ivy Scar and Roulston Scar. *This gives magnificent views westward across the Vale of Mowbray to the Yorkshire Dales: you are unlikely to enjoy them alone however, as countless visitors arrive here after a level stroll from Sutton Bank visitor centre. Youngsters should also be kept under close control hereabouts, some of the nearby drops being alarmingly vertical.*

The dead-level path remains underfoot for virtually a mile around the rim of the escarpment, a spectacular walk with the additional interest of a gliding club to your right. *Along with the White Horse, the Yorkshire Gliding Club is another well-known feature of the Sutton Bank area. The clubhouse is just over to the right, and regularly provides a colourful and animated scene. The graceful movements of gliders are often in evidence in the skies above, more impressive still if one should be towed into the air straight over your head when stood on Roulston Scar. It's the only way of improving on your view! Also well seen are the hairpin bends of the A170's ascent of Sutton Bank, the only main road to tackle the Hambleton Hills. Its fearful reputation is now chiefly a historical one: given a competent driver modern cars have little difficulty, though larger vehicles still occasionally come unstuck.*

Reaching a Cleveland Way sign at the start of a wooded area, leave the edge by an inviting green path heading into the trees. The Cleveland Way follows the line of an old dyke to emerge at a T-junction. *Casten Dyke is an ancient but clearly discernible boundary line of uncertain origin. The Hambleton Hotel is just a minute further along the main road. This is a renowned racehorse training area, with several large establishments nearby.* Turn right along the minor road for about ten minutes, rising imperceptibly to a bend where two enclosed tracks depart the road. *At this point you have good views back over your shoulder 'inland' to the moors, featuring the Bilsdale TV mast, Urra Moor and the crown of Easterside Hill.*

At the junction take the track sharp left, which soon turns right at Shaw's Gate to enter High Wood. Continue on a near straight line along the main track which descends a little at the end, then forks. Of the grassier continuing ways, take that to the right to slant down the few strides to arrive at the chapel at Scotch Corner. *The curiously-sited chapel stands in unrivalled seclusion atop a steep drop to the valley floor. It was built as a World War Two memorial to old boys of nearby Ampleforth College. Above the carved wooden door is a carving of the Madonna and Child. In the neighbourhood of Scotch Corner was fought the Battle of Byland, when in 1322 Edward II was forced to flee from the Scots. Here also the drovers brought their cattle down off the Hambleton Hills on their long journeys south. Busier times for Oldstead!*

Resume down the grassy track, through a gate and descending delightfully down the edge of the wood. *This reveals good views of Cocker Dale on your left amid the southernmost wooded slopes of the Hambleton Hills, and also across to the Howardian Hills and the Wolds.* Leaving the wood, the enclosed cart track continues splendidly down through foliage to emerge onto a rough road. Go briefly right to join a through road at a seat, and turn left to enter Oldstead. *This typical sub-Hambleton village of scattered cottages features the Black Swan pub and a former chapel.*

Immediately after the first buildings on the right take a briefly enclosed path into a field. Slant left up to a gate/stile in a fence corner, then go left on a fenceside track past a small pond. At the end take a gate/stile in front, rather than the inviting green way curving right. Resume along a hedgeside with a nice view left back over the village. *Note that if you continued along the street to the pub, then just before its junction, a signed path enters a field to rise to join the main route along the hedgeside at the top.* At the end drop round the corner to find a stile, and then slant down to a footbridge over a tiny streamlet at the bottom. A path rises up the little bank to a gap in a tall hedgerow. Go through, and from this path junction turn right along the hedgeside. *This vicinity is a riot of springtime colour.*

On emerging from beneath a gorse bank, slant briefly up the bank and cross to a bridle-gate ahead. *On this grassy brow look over to the right for a classic revelation of the White Horse high above pastures and woodland.* Advance on beneath more gorse, and a brief gap precedes a bridle-gate into a lovely enclosed green way. This runs on to join an enclosed cart track, where go right to immediately emerge onto a back road. From a gate/stile opposite, a thin path climbs the field to successive stiles at the top. Cross a small enclosure to a gate opposite, from where a short path descends between houses onto a road.

Turn right through High Kilburn. *This consists of a scattering of attractive dwellings sat lazily back from a green.* At the far end of the green the road runs down to a sharp bend. Take the small gate in front from where a surfaced path drops down the fieldside, with the houses of Kilburn arranged ahead. Crossing a farm track at the bottom, the path runs a hedgerowed course to emerge into the churchyard to finish.

GORMIRE LAKE

A spectacular walk along the Hambleton escarpment and a beautiful circuit of a lake buried in woodland

START *Sutton Bank (SE 515830; YO7 2EH)*

DISTANCE *5¹2 miles (8³4km)*

ORDNANCE SURVEY 1:25,000 MAP
Explorer OL26 - North York Moors West

ACCESS *Start from the National Park Centre, car park.*

Cross the car park on the Sutton Bank side of the visitor centre, joining a firm path that crosses the Cold Kirby road just where it leaves the main road at the rim of Sutton Bank. A very popular and very firm path runs to the right (north). This infallible path runs along the near-level escarpment to quickly reach a viewing platform. *This is proclaimed as the 'Finest view in England': well it's very good, but the finest?* Gormire Lake is already seen in its entirety. You are then joined by a parallel bridleway, and a minute further, a steep path departs left: this will be your return route.

A lovely dead-flat stride now opens out with fantastic views, including all of the lake again. Passing through a short section of woodland the path emerges unannounced on the very crest of Whitestone Cliff, with a seat on the open plinth just to your left. *This early classic moment is the highlight of the walk, though its sheer precipices demand that young children be kept on a tight rein. The limestone cliffs here are of some immensity, and offer rock athletes varied serious climbing opportunities. The waters of Gormire Lake sit amid a deep bowl of greenery dramatically below. Beyond it are the red-roofed villages of Felixkirk and further north, Boltby beneath the backdrop of its forest. Look back south beyond Sutton Bank to appraise the vertical plunge of Roulston Scar. Hambleton Down, on your right, once boasted a race-course, and this remains a major racehorse training area, with several large establishments nearby.*

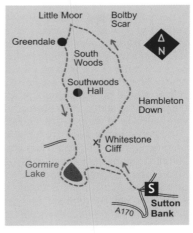

Just strides further, a far more airy plinth looks north along the scar. Beyond Whitestone Cliff you drop slightly to a promontory with another seat to look back along the scar. The separate bridle-way ends here. A huge arc now commences above South Woods, all this superb section being in clear view, and actually completed far more quickly than first imagined. Just after commencing a minor rise above the forest near the far end, a bridleway junction is reached. Signed to Boltby, take the inviting green path striking off left along a gently declining sunken way to a bridle-gate in the forest boundary wall. The path runs pleasantly on past a boulder then drops down through the trees to a forest road. Straight across, the path continues down the forest edge a short way to a bridle-gate out. Slant right down reedy Little Moor to a bridle-gate back into trees. Here a better path slants right down to a T-junction of bridle-paths at the base of the wood.

Turn left through a gate, and a super path follows the fence along the wood bottom towards Greendale. *In springtime there is a glorious display of bluebells here.* Through a bridle-gate drop towards the rear of the farm, but where the bridleway goes right through a gate, instead bear left on a pathless course above a walled wood. You quickly cross to a stile in a fence, and a thin but delectable path heads away through colourful country. It gains a little height as it crosses to the top of a wood, then on through carpets of springtime bluebells to a gorse knoll. Beyond here drop to stiles through a pencil wood, and emerging into open pasture the way invisibly forks. *These fields offer a splendid picture of the outward route, with Whitestone Cliff the main feature.* Bear right past a fence corner and across to a hedge corner, then down its side to a stile onto a grassy track. Go left on this with the hedge, outside the grounds of Southwoods Hall and above a pond to arrive at a junction of ways by the entrance gate at Midge Holm Gate.

Head directly away from the entrance, and through a gate a most enjoyable cart track rises steadily away between hedgerows to reach Southwoods Lodge at a road end. Here turn up to the left on a broad path into the woods. At a near immediate fork go right on the main path which undulates through the trees, and after a slight rise quickly approaches Gormire Lake. *In view during the first mile of the walk, eventual arrival here is a lovely moment, being entirely surrounded by trees. A natural sheet of water, Gormire lies in a deep hollow with neither feeder nor outlet, and at one time was thought to be bottomless!* You now have a choice. *A direct option goes straight ahead to find the lakeshore just to your right and the departure path soon climbing left.*

However, a splendid permissive path undertakes a circuit of the lake. Bearing right at the first fork with the lake still almost hidden, this leads unfailingly all the way round the western shore, a beautiful walk remaining close to the water's edge. Towards the end it merges into a public footpath descending from the right, and just a little further it bears away from the reedy lake end to rise very gently through more open country to meet a firm path. Go left on this to rejoin the shore, very quickly arriving at a path junction. It's penance time now, so take the one climbing steeply right. Quickly entering Garbutt Wood, branch right at a path junction to rise less severely. It levels out to run by a massive, square boulder, then recommences its uphill slant, opening out from the trees to restore the big views and ultimately rejoin the outward path on the scarp. The top of Sutton Bank is now only five minutes along to the right. It is also worth crossing the road with care to visit the topograph with views along the escarpment to Roulston Scar.

RIEVAULX ABBEY

Easy walking above and below Ryedale's wooded slopes, not forgetting a truly magnificent monastic ruin

START *Rievaulx (SE 575849; YO62 5LB)*

DISTANCE *6 miles (9½km)*

ORDNANCE SURVEY 1:25,000 MAP
Explorer OL26 - North York Moors West

ACCESS *Start from the village centre. Car park (refund for abbey visitors), roadside parking. Alternative start: Old Byland.*

Rievaulx Abbey dates from the 12th century and vies with that other great Yorkshire house of the Cistercians, Fountains Abbey, in the beauty of its wooded environs. There is however a very imposing grandeur here that is virtually unparalleled: perhaps not surprisingly, the abbey took over a century to build. It is now in the care of English Heritage. High on the hillside above (reached by continuing up the lane through the hamlet - note the thatched cottages) are the delightfully laid out Rievaulx Terraces, complete with two temples. Created by the Duncombe family in the 18th century, the National Trust now maintains that site.

From the abbey take the road north into the hamlet, and after a handful of buildings take a gate on the left ('footpath to Bow Bridge'). Cross a stable yard and a paddock before continuing away alongside a hedge. *Just over it are the scant remains of a canal*

47

that brought quarried stone to the abbey construction site. A grassy path heads away with a hedge on the right, then along a fenceside. This straight line leads to the bank of the River Rye. A sketchy path heads upstream, but with Bow Bridge visible ahead, leave the river for a bridle-gate onto an enclosed track which drops down to the shapely bridge. Shortly after it, before the track starts to scale the wooded bank, take a gate on the right and a path heads away alongside a fence beneath a scrubby bank. At the end the river is rejoined, and traced on boardwalks through a steep wooded bank. Emerging, forsake the river again as the path crosses straight over the pasture to a gate onto a farm road.

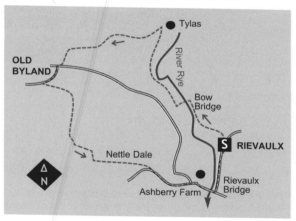

Follow this access road right to its demise above Tylas Farm. Without dropping to the farm, instead take a gate on the left and ascend a track climbing steeply to Tylas Barn. *This climb opens up views over wooded Ryedale, while at the top the barn bears a massive red pantiled roof.* Beyond the barn the track runs to a junction at the head of tiny Oxendale. From a stile in front a scant field-path heads directly away, rising imperceptibly in a straight line along field edges. At the end of the fourth - with no further stiles - turn left in another straight line with an old hedgeside, through a gateway and dropping to a stile onto a road. Turn right then quickly left to enter Old Byland at a North Riding guidepost.

Old Byland is set on a plateau with deep-cut wooded valleys on three sides. This sleepy, attractive village stands back from a large sloping green. Here the monks of Furness Abbey settled until problems arose due to their proximity to Rievaulx. As a result they moved four miles south and established Byland Abbey (visited on WALK 9). Hidden away is the small but delightful church of All Saints, with some Norman work and a simple timber-framed roof.

After descending the green the road becomes enclosed before leaving the village. Just after the village sign take a bridle-gate on the left, and a thin path doubles back through trees and scrub to cross a small dry valley. On the other side it rises past a low line of limestone outcrops for a delightful walk through the trees. With the valley opening out into a deep wooded dale below, the path suddenly quits this scene at a bridle-gate on the right. Cross over a track to a gate in the left corner. *Pause to look back to a good prospect of the village, with open views ahead too.* Head away along two hedgesides to drop to a bridle-gate into Callister Wood.

A charming hollowed path drops left, and absorbing an early path from the right, slants all the way to a footbridge out of the wood. Cross to a stile just ahead, then over a track and through a bridle-gate in a wooded corner. Behind are sturdy stepping-stones on a smaller stream. This delightful corner marks your arrival in Nettle Dale: joining a wide forest track just behind, turn left for a splendid half-mile through the dale. *Within this attractive nature reserve a string of ponds on your left is enjoyed by waterfowl.* The track emerges onto a road: turn left to soon arrive at Ashberry Farm, keeping right at the fork (another North Riding roadsign). The farm makes a lovely picture, as does the scene by the cottage at Rievaulx Bridge, five minutes further. Across the bridge turn left along the road back to the beckoning abbey. Part way on, a short section of path offers an unofficial stroll with the Rye.

At Old Byland

BOLTBY SCAR

A lively climb to a delectable stroll along the Boltby skyline

START Boltby (SE 492866; YO7 2DY)

DISTANCE $5\frac{1}{2}$ miles ($8\frac{3}{4}$km)

ORDNANCE SURVEY 1:25,000 MAP
Explorer OL26 - North York Moors West

ACCESS Start from the village centre, roadside parking.
Also a useful roadside parking area above east end of village.

Boltby is an immensely attractive village in the shadow of the Hambleton Hills. With tidy stone cottages under red pantile roofs, its enviable setting renders it near perfect. The modest church of the Holy Trinity sports a small bell-cote, while a trekking centre takes advantage of the many bridleways in the neighbourhood. From the church head east along the road, past a tiny stone-arched footbridge and superfluous ford, and the village hall, to a tiny grassy triangle just outside the old Methodist chapel. Here turn right along a 'no through road'. This downgrades to a rougher byway by the time it reaches a ford and footbridge.

The Boltby Scar skyline awaits as the lane eventually expires at a field. A thin path heads straight up the side, and at the bracken level runs firmly right to a gate/stile into the foot of the wood. *There is a good view back over the village backed by the extensive Boltby Forest.* The path rises, part-sunken, soon leaving the trees on the right to arrive at a bridleway junction on a little knoll. *By now you have extensive views over the plains to the eastern hills of the Yorkshire Dales.* Turn up to the left, on a path climbing alongside a part-sunken way to a bridle-gate out of the trees.

The path slants right up the reedy pasture of Little Moor to another such gate into the edge of a plantation. A broad path rises directly up the side, over a forest road on a minor knoll, then curving up right - still with the old wall - to soon level out. Here the wall finally parts company, things open out, and a big rock suggests a halt. This level section leads to a bridle-gate in a wall out of the forest. Part sunken yet again, a lovely green path slants up the edge of the moor to gain the Cleveland Way path running along the lofty Hambleton escarpment. *First turn and look back south along the edge above the great arc of South Woods.*

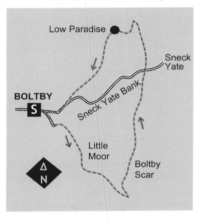

Turn left, heading north and still rising slightly to soon leave the plantation behind and arrive above Boltby Scar on the summit of the walk. *The grand path along here makes a splendid view-point, with Boltby nestling at your feet far below; the Hambleton Hills stretching away both north and south; and on a clear day the mountains of the Yorkshire Dales beyond the flat Vale of York. There is a great sweep of moorland eastwards too, featuring the Bilsdale TV mast, the Hawnby Hills and some Tabular Hills' edges.*

A brief section follows with a wall to the left above an old quarry, beyond which a broad grassy way remains with the wall to the prominent High Barn in its surround of trees. A little beyond it the way drops gently down, and as a wall replaces the fence it angles further left to drop to a gate in the wall ahead. Just through it you meet the Sneck Yate road. *This is almost the high point of a minor road over the Hambleton Hills.* Cross straight over the road and head along a splendid woodland path. At the far end it emerges to run on as a fine green way to join the High Paradise farm road. Turn left to commence the return.

Passing a pair of Legoland cottages you double back downhill briefly, but then quickly fork right down the drive to Low Paradise. Turn left down to the house, passing along the front to a stile that sends a briefly-enclosed path down into a field. Descend a fence-side to a bridle-gate at the bottom, then steeply down a field to a stone slab bridge on a tiny stream. Across it bear left into a field, and going downstream the thin path slants up to a stile by a gate towards the top. Joining a forest road, cross straight over and go left up a good path behind.

Soon re-emerging at a gate/stile, follow the right-hand fence away alongside an old line of hawthorns. Remain with the fence beneath a small plantation to a gate/stile into a large pasture. The thinnest of trods contours across this, initially slightly rising, then nearing the wall below and passing beneath a small, enclosed reservoir. When the wall ends slant gently up towards the end to a stile onto a farm drive. Go left down it to a road, then turn right for a short five minutes back into Boltby. *This road affords a near complete picture of the circuit just enjoyed.*

Springtime at Boltby

HAMBLETON DROVE ROAD

A colourful climb to a good section of a famous old road

START *Kepwick (SE 468909; YO7 4BH)*

DISTANCE *5^1$_2$ miles (8^3$_4$km)*

ORDNANCE SURVEY 1:25,000 MAP
Explorer OL26 - North York Moors West

ACCESS *Start from the village centre. Small car park by church.*

Kepwick is an unassuming little village, totally linear with wide-cropped verges along the road and some lovely cottages set sedately back from it. Its modest church has a tiny bell-cote, and is a private memorial chapel dating from 1894. At the other end of the village a drive runs along to Kepwick Hall. Leave by the Cowesby road past the church, and just beyond the de-restriction sign take a gate on the left. A part sunken old way rises by gorse bushes to a gate in the wall at the top, from where a good path rises left through bracken and rhododendrons. It swings round to the right and up a deep groove to emerge onto more open ground, fading but merging into a broad green way on Pen Hill.

Ahead is the Hambleton skyline you will soon be joining. Already the hardest work is behind, and the path continues by a wall along a lovely open pasture. At the end a gate at a kink in the wall takes you to the other side to gain height up a narrow strip of scrubby moorland. Leaving the trees and scrub the path curves left

53

with the wall and rises through a hollow and out onto Gallow Hill, then grandly along to a gate in a fence at a corner of Boltby Forest.

At this bridleway junction turn immediately left through a gate in the wall, from where a super grassy track heads away across the bilberry-draped moor. *Big views look out to the Vale of Mowbray, while Kepwick and its hall are prominent.* The way curves up to a distinct groove visible ahead, then rises to run along a well-defined edge. This soon levels out and curves inland to join a fence leading to a gate in a wall to join the Hambleton Drove Road.

The old drove road is followed to the north for a longish half-mile. *This classic moorland highway has been in use since Bronze Age times, though its fame springs from the busy droving days centred around the 18th century. Then it was the favoured way of Scottish drovers* and their herds of cattle heading for the markets further south, avoiding the costly turnpike roads. The drovers clung to the high Hambletons from Scarth Nick to Oldstead, though some parts are now surfaced. The remaining green road is unsurpassed for sheer atmosphere. *Opposite is a boundary stones inscribed 'CT 1770'.*

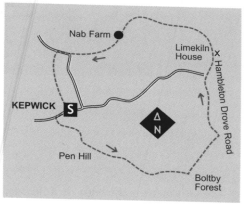

Turning left on it, glorious strides lead on over the open moorland, though the left-hand wall never leaves your side. *Massive views look west to Great Whernside, Buckden Pike and Penhill in the Yorkshire Dales. Ahead, meanwhile, on your old road is the scarred western flank of Black Hambleton.* Dropping gently down, a second boundary stone precedes the crossing of an old road that is surfaced on the Kepwick side. Firmer now, your way continues down to a minor dip. *The sparse piles of stones here are all that remain of Limekiln House, a former drovers' inn.*

Immediately past the ruins, a gate in the wall on the left sees you heading back for the valley. A splendid green path descends with a wall through colourful terrain. *Well over to the left note the site of the substantial former Kepwick Quarry, while down below is the village and its lovely surroundings.* A footpath stays by the wall when the old way undertakes a curve to outflank the steeper gradient here. At the bottom a small plantation sees you leave the wall to drop to a gate off the moor by an old limekiln. The fainter track drops down a field to cross a beck, from where a firmer track curves around to Nab Farm. Keep left of the buildings onto the farm road, which leads down to a bend of the Kepwick-Silton road. *During this stroll a glance up to the left will identify the course of a 19th century tramway that brought stone down from the quarry.*

Turn right on the road for a couple of minutes to the next bend, where take a gate on the left. Head directly away to find a stile in a recessed corner. Head away over a minor knoll and drop to a footbridge in the opposite corner. Across tree-lined Bridge Beck bear left to a stile onto an enclosed cart track. *This is the old quarry tramway route.* From a gate opposite bear right to a hedge-stile, then slant up the field behind. As the invisible path forks here, rise left to a gate in the fence on the near side of the farm buildings. Finish by rising up a paddock to a gate back onto the road in Kepwick.

Looking west from under the Drove Road

HAWNBY HILLS

An exhilarating circuit of two shapely hills,
with beautiful views over Ryedale and Bilsdale

START Hawnby (SE 543898; YO62 5QS)

DISTANCE 5$\frac{3}{4}$ miles (9$\frac{1}{4}$km)

ORDNANCE SURVEY 1:25,000 MAP
Explorer OL26 - North York Moors West

ACCESS Start from the T-junction outside the hotel. Limited
roadside parking. Further parking by bridge at foot of village.
An alternative start is Moor Gate, where the route crosses the
Osmotherley road mid-walk. •OPEN ACCESS - see page 8.

Hawnby village boasts an enviable setting in the heart of
upper Ryedale, and is the largest community above Helmsley. This
quiet backwater rises steeply from near the river up onto the
lower slopes of Hawnby Hill: once a Quaker stronghold, it seems to
have let a few decades pass by. All Saints church is set in splendid
isolation by the wooded riverbank, with Norman work and the
tombs of generations of the Tancreds of nearby Arden Hall. The
upper section of the village contains the Inn at Hawnby, a small
green and lovely cottages. Hawnby Hill and Easterside Hill are
twin-like outliers of the Tabular Hills, which occur regularly across
the southern moors. With their upturned boat appearance, these
two betray their colleagues which drop steeply only to the north.

Leave the junction outside the inn by an enclosed cart track rising between cottages directly above. By a barn at the top it emerges into a field, which ascend to locate a bridle-gate in a kink at the top. From it a clear path ascends steeply through bracken on Hawnby Hill's lower slopes. Meeting one rising from the left, the gradients of this super route soon ease, and gentler walking leads across the moor to the start of the crest of the hill. Passing through a nick above Hawnby Hill Crag down to the left, a modern cairn is soon reached at around 965ft/294m. *Though not quite the highest point, it now reveals the modest ridge ahead.* This ensuing half-mile is quite simply superb, in both your immediate surroundings and the all-round views. *Partly wooded slopes fall to the east and rougher slopes to the west. The Ryedale scene is outstanding, especially the uppermost section backed by Black Hambleton, while neighbouring Easterside Hill is inevitably prominent.*

The highest point of 977ft/298m comes just after passing through the vestiges of a wall that crosses the ridge. Resuming north, the ridge soon dissolves and you simply continue straight off the end. *Note that a less steep, sunken path may be found curving down the right flank just short of the end.* The main path spirals briefly steeply down to quickly level out and run more thinly on to meet a grassy cart track. The thin trod crosses straight over, at once broadening to run a nice course on and then down to the open road at a cattle-grid at Moor Gate.

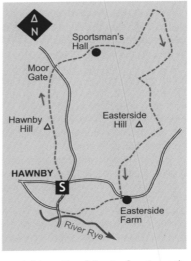

Over the cattle-grid go sharp right on the drive to Sportsman's Hall. Without entering, remain on the moor on a path running left with the wall. Within a couple of minutes turn through a bridle-gate in the wall, and drop down a slim field to a gate just below.

Bear left away from the house to your right, crossing towards the far end of the field. Pass through a long crumbled wall and drop more steeply left to a gate in the bottom corner, and a path slants right down the wooded bank to a footbridge on Ladhill Beck.

Across, take the path running right between the beck and a fence above, quickly reaching a bridle-gate in the fence. A good path rises past a lone boulder up the moorland slope to meet a grassy track. Turn left on this, rising gently as far as a fork after 250 paces. Keep right here, maintaining the gentle rise to ascend to a wall, going left with it to quickly reach a gate in it. Through this the track resumes on further open moorland, diverging from the wall to rise very steadily up the moor. Before long you will meet a similar track doubling back right. Turn down this, crossing to join the nearby wall on the other side of the moor. This abandoned track now bears right to shadow the wall on a very gradual descent. Ahead, Easterside Hill looms large.

Before too long, with a solitary tree on your right, a bridleway comes out from the fields at a gate on the left. Turn right on this into a small hollow, from where the suddenly thin but very clear path continues away through otherwise dense heather. On gaining the gentle brow just ahead it forks at a tiny cairn. Bear left here, locating the improving path that runs towards the wall ahead under Easterside Hill. The thin path drops slightly right to meet the wall at a gate where it passes through, but you might veer left to retain height to meet the wall. On its near side a super path is followed left all the way along the wallside under Easterside Hill, enjoying gorgeous Bilsdale views.

As path and wall/fence start to drop more towards the road, locate a stile at a fence corner where grassy pasture replaces moorland over the wall. Ascending a few paces from it the path then turns left, soon being abandoned by the fence to commence a slant up across the flank of the hill on a superb old path. Dead straight, it narrows at the top as it swings up to the right and onto a plateau well to the south of Easterside Hill's high point.

Super views look westwards over the Hawnby area, and east-wards over the wooded surroundings of the meeting of Ryedale and Bilsdale, with Roppa Edge prominent across the latter. The path continues across to quickly commence its descent, with a marked swing left seeing it slant more gently across the flank, dropping at the end to a fence-stile off the hill. Drop down the fieldside towards Easterside Farm, and at the end deflect briefly right to a gate/stile onto a road.

Cross straight over to a gate and drop half-right to a hidden stile into the top of a wood, just left of a telegraph pole. Descend a moist section to a stile at the bottom, and continue down a large, sloping pasture alongside a tiny stream. Crossing it near the bottom, resume briefly down its other side to find a footbridge at a nice curve on the larger Ladhill Beck, which you cross for the second time on the walk. Head directly away through two flat fields with a gateway midway. At the end a gate puts you onto a road junction by the cottages at Hawnby Bridge on the Rye.

The Rye is the major river of the western part of the Moors, flowing 16 unspoilt miles to leave the National Park at Helmsley. Several other rivers are absorbed in the Vale of Pickering before its own identity is lost in the Derwent, just short of Malton. Turn briefly right to a T-junction, noting the shop/tearoom in the row of cottages ahead and a former Wesleyan chapel of 1770. The walk concludes with a steep climb to the right.

Looking west to Black Hambleton from Hawnby Hill Crag

BLACK HAMBLETON

*A grand climb to Black Hambleton and the Drove Road,
with almost entirely moorland surroundings*

START Snilesworth (SE 510944; YO62 5QD)

DISTANCE 6$\frac{1}{2}$ miles (10$\frac{1}{2}$km)

ORDNANCE SURVEY 1:25,000 MAP
Explorer OL26 - North York Moors West

ACCESS Start from the Hawnby-Osmotherley road just south of
Low Cote Farm. Parking area where the road meets Wheat Beck
between steep gradients. An alternative start is the car park at
Square Corner, Oakdale Head. •OPEN ACCESS - see page 8.

Apart from good paths underfoot and the lack of navigational
details, the great pleasure of this walk is the diversity of scenery,
nearby and distant. At various stages all points of the compass
appear, disappear and then return, but there is never a complete
all-round vista. This cat and mouse game is rather enjoyable!

The scattered community of Snilesworth stands at the very
head of Ryedale: above it are only the moors. Low Cote, on a sharp
bend of the road, hides the phonebox and is probably the nearest
thing to a focal point. From the car park cross the adjacent farm
bridge over Wheat Beck and follow the Locker Farm drive up
through the field. As it doubles back up to the left, branch right
through a bridle-gate. An old hollowed way slants up into a field,

continuing more faintly up the wallside to a gate onto the open moor. This is the point to which you shall return. Take the thin path climbing left near the wall. On gentler ground a track comes in from a gate to take over, and gaining the steep bank ahead, it becomes a stonier dog-leg up the steep Locker Bank.

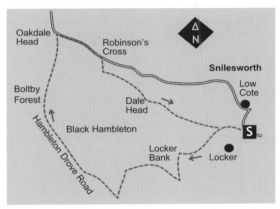

The climb is worthy of punctuation in order to appreciate the rapidly expanding view over the infant Rye, with patchwork fields rising to a moorland background. Nearing the top the switchback ridge of the Cleveland Hills is seen to the north, with Carlton Moor quickly joined by Cringle Moor and Cold Moor. Eastwards are the abrupt escarpments of the Tabular Hills. At the top of the zigzag a steeper, direct pull sees you gain the moor top at a T-junction. Turn right along this level track which eventually swings round left to cross the plateau to drop slightly onto the Hambleton Drove Road at White Gill Head. *For a note on the drove road see page 54.*

Double back right along the stony surface of this wide old highway, which with its accompanying wall rises imperceptibly over Black Hambleton to reach a substantial cairn. *Beyond the dead-flat vale rises the long line of the Pennine Hills, with Great and Little Whernsides, Buckden Pike and Penhill all distinctive on a clear day. Black Hambleton is the highest and northernmost of the Hambleton Hills: beyond the divide of Oakdale Head and upper Ryedale the Cleveland Hills take over.*

From the cairn the track descends fairly rapidly, but soon eases out again alongside the plantation. *Ahead, the red roofs of Osmotherley are conspicuous, while Carlton, Cringle and Cold Moors briefly return in shapely style.* The way levels out again to join the unfenced Osmotherley-Hawnby road at Square Corner, Oakdale Head. *Just before this, at a gate, you pass the Grayhall Stone, an inscribed boundary stone.* Turn right along the road, with a reasonable verge to assist. The boundary stone of Robinson's Cross occupies a modest brow alongside three little rowan trees, where an improved verge takes over. Within minutes of this, leave the road by a good track to the right, which leads unfailingly down to the remains of Dale Head Farm.

Briefly leaving moorland, drop down between the ruinous buildings. *In a relatively short period of time this old farm has gone from dereliction to renovation and back to dereliction.* From a gate beneath the buildings, head away with a fence on the right to drop to a wooden farm bridge on a small beck. Across, a path rises away back onto moorland, quickly levelling out to run on well above the beck down to your left. It leads unfailingly back to the moor-gate, from where opening steps are now retraced.

Looking over Kepwick from the Drove Road

ABOVE OSMOTHERLEY

*Easy walking around the colourful little dales
linking Osmotherley with the high moors*

START *Osmotherley (SE 456972; DL6 3AA)*

DISTANCE *5 miles (8km)*

ORDNANCE SURVEY 1:25,000 MAP
Explorer OL26 - North York Moors West

ACCESS *Start from the village centre, roadside parking.
Northallerton-Stokesley bus (not Sunday).*

   Osmotherley has a highly attractive village centre where a
small green marks the meeting of roads lined by stone cottages,
the main street sloping throughout its length. On the green is a
sturdy market cross, next to which is a stone table where John
Wesley once preached: just around the back is his early Methodist
chapel of 1754. Almost everything has a central position, with the
church of St Peter showing traces of Norman work, and three pubs.
There are also tearooms, shop, fish-shop, youth hostel and an
annual agricultural show. As starting point for the infamous Lyke
Wake Walk, Osmotherley has an indefinable ramblers' atmosphere.
   Leave the village centre by the Swainby road which climbs due
north, passing a former chapel and some lovely cottages. When the
climb eases out advance just a short way past the de-restriction
sign then turn right down a rough, enclosed track. This drops to a

ford and bridge on Cod Beck, then climbs steeply away. As it forks keep straight up to the farm above. Pass through a series of gates to keep left of the farm and escape into a field above, then ascend the hedgeside to a gate at the top onto a green lane. *This is a good moment to look back over the village to the Vale of Mowbray.*

Turn right on the green lane, through a gate/stile to enjoy a colourful, enclosed level stroll. Just as it starts to drop gently away take a stile on the left, cross a horse track to a small gate and a path climbs away alongside an old wall. Through a gate/stile at the top the going eases and most of your work is done. *Big moorland surrounds are dominated by Black Hambleton across to the right: its prow is very much the dominant feature of the walk.*

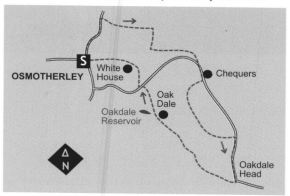

Advance along the fieldside with the wall, but just short of the corner gate, instead take a stile in a gateway on your right to enter open country. *This offers good views to Black Hambleton, across your upland circuit around the deep bowl of Slape Stones Beck.* A little path goes left to meet a grassy cart track, which runs along a fenceside to emerge onto a surfaced back road: a couple of green ways on your right offer minor short-cuts part way along. Turning right you immediately join the Osmotherley-Hawnby road.

Turn left as far as Chequers. *Chequers Farm at Slape Stones was once an inn serving cattle drovers: note the sign affixed to the outside wall. Though refreshments and a farm shop replaced it, today all is quiet.* Immediately beyond it take a wallside track to the right back onto the moor. When the wall turns off left after a gate/stile, go with it on a lesser track, which beyond a few reeds joins a better grassy track rising from the main one. Go left on this, rising slightly and tracing that wall all the way, over a heathery brow and gently down to a gate. Through this a firmer track is joined and followed left, still with the wall back onto the road.

Turn right, and with a verge all the way this road crosses the moor to a popular car park at a sharp bend at Square Corner at Oakdale Head under Black Hambleton. Here you join the Cleveland Way which will lead all the way back to Osmotherley. This takes the firm path dropping right across the moor, through bracken and heather with Osmotherley seen straight ahead. Soon becoming flagged and pitched, it drops down into Oak Dale. *Oak Dale takes a deep bite into the shoulder of Black Hambleton to the south-east.* Entering trees, in front is the site of Oakdale Upper Reservoir, drained in 2014 and returning to a more natural appearance. Over a small footbridge an access road is joined, and leads out past the former reservoir and down to the lone house of Oak Dale Farm.

Resume down this rough road, crossing a bridge at a sheltered corner with a faint glimpse of the surviving Oakdale Lower Reservoir. It then climbs steeply and opens out to run along to a road in front of a lone house. Drop very briefly left then take a farm drive climbing right. It quickly eases and runs pleasantly on to swing left down towards White House Farm. Just before it your path contours across a steep field bottom on the right, passing above the farm. At the corner descend two fieldsides to a bridle-gate into woodland. The path drops down to an access road at the bottom, across which is a footbridge over Cod Beck. A steep climb up the wooded bank behind soon deposits you into a field with Osmotherley just in front. An enclosed, flagged path crosses a couple of fields to a hedgerowed snicket onto a back lane. Take the private-looking snicket opposite to pass the Methodist chapel and emerge in novel fashion into the village centre.

At Chequers

65

WHORLTON CASTLE

A gentle walk that might be subtitled 'The Bluebell Way'

START *Swainby (SE 477020; DL6 3ED)*

DISTANCE *6 miles (9$\frac{1}{2}$km)*

ORDNANCE SURVEY 1:25,000 MAP
Explorer OL26 - North York Moors West

ACCESS *Start from the village centre, roadside parking.*
Northallerton-Stokesley bus (not Sundays).

Swainby is a delightful village centred on a stream running its entire length, and overlooked by massed ranks of high woodland. There are two pubs here, the Blacksmiths Arms and the Black Horse, along with a shop and WCs. The church of the Holy Cross stands imposingly in the centre, its tall spire overtopping all. Also gathered around are the former Whorlton Parochial School of 1856, and the Whorlton Recreation Rooms of 1919, now the village hall. A restored pinfold enjoys a floral surround by the bridge.

Head south up the High Street from the bridge, past the church on the other bank and eventually out of the village. Past the Scugdale turning, remain on the road for some while as it rises gently as Shepherd Hill through enviable scattered suburbia before swinging right. Here go straight on up a hedgerowed cart track, which maintains the steady rise to enter Clain Wood. Turn sharp left on the route of the Cleveland Way, and a grand, firm path runs along the edge of the wood. Entering deeper woodland, the first of the promised bluebells leap into action. Keep on this undulating way until the Cleveland Way departs at a kissing-gate on the left. *Ahead over the fields are lovely views into Scugdale driving its deep wedge between Live Moor and Whorlton Moor.*

Your way is straight on to leave the wood at a corner gate just ahead. Head away with a fence on your right, and from a gate at the end a faint way heads off across a sloping field, rising slightly right to a gate ahead. Advance on through open pasture with woods to either side and high moorland ahead. Through two further pastures, at the end a track forms crossing a tiny stream, becoming briefly enclosed to curve up onto a back lane. Go briefly right uphill to its terminus at Harfa Bank Farm. The continuing way turns sharp left, now unsurfaced as it drops between hedgerows and along to Harfa House ahead.

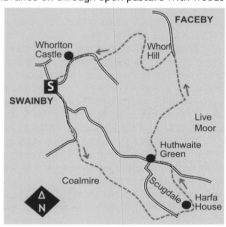

The road seems to end at the farm, but from a gate ahead a firm continuation resumes. Follow this for only a minute, however, then from a stile on the left at the end of the first field, double sharply back across to a stile beneath the rear of the farm. Now turn right down the fenceside, and when trees take over bear left across a reedy pasture to a gate/stile beneath a telegraph pole. Head slightly left across an open pasture with a hedge-line just to your left. At the far end a stile sends a faint path slanting left down a part wooded bank, and down to Scugdale Beck with a footbridge just a few paces downstream. Across, a thin path rises left to a stile out of the trees, then up to a stile at the top left of the field. Cross a further field top to a stile onto a hedgerowed back road, and go left to quickly reach a junction at Huthwaite Green.

At the T-junction leave the road by a fenced path rising to a wood. *At the top note the grassy embankment of an old tramway scaling the slope in front: this is the course of the mineral line that served the ironstone mines.* Your way rises more gently left beneath the base of the wood, emerging at a bridle-gate to run on above gorse and spoil heaps to a corner of the wood. Don't follow the main path up into the trees, but take the left-hand bridle-gate and head along the gorse-filled field top beneath the wood. At the end a bridle-gate puts you into the trees, and a short path rises left onto a broad forest path. Turn left along this, absorbing a lower path near a Whorlton/Faceby boundary stone. At a fork a little further, take the left branch slanting down to a bridle-gate out of the wood.

Ahead is a fine open prospect of tree-capped Whorl Hill, with more distant Roseberry Topping straight ahead. Maintain the slant down the field to a gate onto the broad track of Bank Lane. Turn down the track leading to Faceby, but unless desperate for the pub, don't follow it all the way. *Faceby is a small village featuring the Sutton Arms, the church of St Mary Magdalen with a small bell turret, and a mix of attractive cottages and modern dwellings.*

The lane rises to become surfaced at a knoll by High Farm. Just a few paces further, at the first house on the left, the wooded slopes of Whorl Hill begin. Take a stile and cross the edge of the lawn to a stile into the corner of the wood. *On a bright spring day, the carpets of bluebells throughout these woods are peerless.* Take the path climbing steeply straight up the wood side. Part way up it merges into a broader path. Continue up until it levels out at a junction with a similar track. Turn left here, and an undulating path winds around the western flank of the hill. *Rather than leaving the bluebells behind, it meanders through the most beautiful walking imaginable. In addition to all this, you also find open views out to the villages of the Cleveland Plain.* At the end it merges with a path from the right to drop to the opposite corner of the wood.

A kissing-gate puts you onto another path, going left through a second kissing-gate outside Whorl Hill Farm, crossing a track and heading away on a briefly enclosed green way above the house. Emerging at a gate, keep straight on a faint little path, improving along the field top for a nice stroll looking down on the flat plains beyond bluebell slopes. From a kissing-gate at the end continue along a fieldside with Whorlton Castle ahead. From a stile at the end, follow a grass track across a paddock to emerge onto a bend of Whorlton Lane. Bear right, passing both church and castle. *A stile gives access to the church of the Old Holy Cross which initially appears intact, but soon proves otherwise. It dates back to the 12th century: while the chancel and 600-year old tower are preserved, the arches of the nave stand forlorn. The chancel is viewed through a window in the door, the finest feature being a wooden effigy of Nicholas de Meynell of Whorlton Castle, who died in 1322. A replacement church was built in 1877 in Swainby.*

Whorlton Castle's site was occupied by the Romans, whose coins and pottery have been unearthed locally. The present remains are the Meynell's 14th century castle. The gatehouse is most impressive as you approach, and bears the arms of the Meynells, Greys and Darcys. The castle has a link with Mary, Queen of Scots, for Lord Darnley's family owned it at the time of their marriage: it later saw Civil War action. Ambitious plans are afoot to restore it as holiday accommodation. Leaving the castle, Swainby appears just ahead. Reaching the edge of the village, a nicer finish can be made just before a bend by the first house. Cross a tiny bridge on the right and follow an enclosed path along a tiny streamside. *Part way on it crosses the distinct course of the old ironstone railway serving Scugdale.* The path emerges back onto the street adjacent to the Black Horse.

Whorlton Castle

CARLTON MOOR

Verdant Scugdale separates two high moorland sections

START *Carlton Bank (NZ 523030; TS9 7JH)*

DISTANCE *7 miles (11¼km)*

ORDNANCE SURVEY 1:25,000 MAP
Explorer OL26 - North York Moors West

ACCESS *Start from Lord Stones Country Park on summit of Carlton-Chop Gate road above Carlton Bank. Car park.*

The summit of Carlton Bank boasts an intelligently hidden café and car park. The former is a particular boon to long distance walkers as it offers the only on-route refreshment to Cleveland Wayfarers between Osmotherley and Kildale; and to Coast to Coasters between Ingleby Arncliffe and the Lion Inn at Blakey. From the car park entrance turn briefly right on the road, meeting the Cleveland Way path crossing it. Go left on this flagged course rising through bracken alongside a plantation to quickly meet a broad, stony track, a former gliding club access road: turn left.

Through a gate it commences a pleasant gentle slant through bracken across the moor. *Look back north to Roseberry Topping and Middlesbrough, while neighbouring Cringle Moor is straight across.* As the track eases up at a pronounced right bend just past an old quarry, a clear path bears off left to commence a delightful level stroll through the heather and along a brow. Terminating at a broad track, identify a much slimmer continuation straight ahead, this thin trod running a good course through heather to decline gently to a meeting of hard tracks. Advance straight on this newly merged way beneath boulders to the left. The track makes a long, steady descent to Brian's Pond, visible well in advance. *During this the views include the long line of Cold Moor over to the left, leading the eye into Raisdale, running into Bilsdale, and ahead to Whorlton Moor overtopped by Black Hambleton. Brian's Pond is a lovely reed-fringed pool right by the track.*

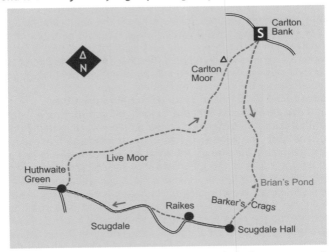

Immediately after the pond is a major fork, but your way is a less obvious but still very clear bridle-path branching right just short of the fork. This runs to a smaller, kidney-shaped pool, beyond which the path swings left and soon forks. Keep straight on (right) to very quickly gain a section of Barker's Crags on the well-defined edge overlooking Scugdale. *This is a real moment to linger and absorb the supreme loveliness of Scugdale, deep and green and thrusting into the heart of the moors. The nearest buildings below are your objective of Scugdale Hall.*

Paths run in from either side on this edge, and faced with dense bracken slopes below, advance very briefly left on a thin

71

trod which slants gently down to a grooved way. Parallel behind is a sunken bridleway slanting down to a hidden bridle-gate in a fence. *Look back up to appraise the great length of the scattered boulders of Barker's Crags: some sections are substantial enough to attract rock climbers.* The path continues its slant down to the right end of a section of wall, then down through a bridle-gate below to join a rough road by Scugdale Hall. Turn right along the drive which at once becomes surfaced to begin a quiet, pleasant journey down Scugdale to Huthwaite Green.

At the first farm along the road (Raikes Farm) there is a chance to cut out a road section. Take a stile on the bend, immediately left of the buildings, and a track crosses the field to a gate/stile. Now slant down the large field to a pair of stiles part way on, beyond a cluster of modern barns. Resume on the other side along to a footbridge on a tree-lined stream, a delightful bluebell dell. From a stile up the other side cross to a stone gap-stile back onto the road, and turn right to continue to Huthwaite Green.

Scugdale was once mined for alum, jet and ironstone, with a railway taking the latter out of the valley. Whilst walking down the lane note the extensive line of spoil heaps on the opposite slope indicating the line of old workings. At Huthwaite Green you pick up the route of the Cleveland Way for the remainder of the walk. Work in recent years has seen much change in the nature of the path: expect lengthy sections to be on man-made stone ways.

At the T-junction leave the road by a fenced path rising to a wood. *At the top note the grassy embankment of the old tramway in front.* Your way rises more gently left, emerging to run between wood and spoil heaps to a pair of bridle-gates at the far end. From the right one a steep, well-pitched climb leads quickly up through the trees onto the foot of Live Moor. *Immediately open views expand, featuring distant Roseberry Topping, with Carlton Moor itself projecting high ahead.*

The path rises ever gradually before finally levelling out beneath a cairn to your right, to run along the crest of Live Moor. *From Huthwaite Green to Carlton Moor the steep western scarp contrasts well with the heather carpet of the moor top to the right. This western scarp is littered with long-abandoned jet and alum workings.* The highest point of Live Moor is marked by a sprawling cairn, with views down into Scugdale. A modest descent is made to a section with an 'A/F' boundary stone and only Scugdale views, before a short pull onto the edge of Carlton Moor. The end of an old glider runway is reached and this shadows you left along the edge. *For many decades the Newcastle & Teesside (later Carlton Moor) Gliding Club operated from the very crest of Carlton Moor. Only in the 21st century did the club fold, the eyesore buildings being dismantled in 2013 to help restore the site.* Height is only very gradually gained now as the path leads unfailingly to the Ordnance Survey column and boundary stone at the moor's summit.

Carlton Moor rises to a well-defined top perched above a steep fall to the Cleveland Plain. At 1338ft/408m this is a summit on which to linger - select a heathery couch beneath the exposed top and see how many communities can be identified with the aid of an OS map. The nearest, appropriately, is Carlton, literally at your feet. The final descent is swift, the end already in sight. The path keeps firmly above old alum workings to drop down to their right, then it winds less steeply left to drop to a kissing-gate onto the stony track near the start. Cross straight over and return as you began to the road at Carlton Bank. From a bridle-gate opposite you can opt to follow a grassy path to the WCs and the car park.

Boundary stone on the summit of Carlton Moor

CRINGLE MOOR

A colourful circuit of Cringle Moor and its hinterland

START *Carlton Bank (NZ 523030; TS9 7JH)*

DISTANCE *5$\frac{1}{2}$ miles (8$\frac{3}{4}$km)*

ORDNANCE SURVEY 1:25,000 MAP
Explorer OL26 - North York Moors West

ACCESS *Start from Lord Stones Country Park on summit of Carlton-Chop Gate road above Carlton Bank. Car park.*

The summit of Carlton Bank boasts an intelligently hidden café and car park. The former is a particular boon to long distance walkers as it offers the only on-route refreshment to Cleveland Wayfarers between Osmotherley and Kildale; and to Coast to Coasters between Ingleby Arncliffe and the Lion Inn at Blakey.

Leave the car park by the rear, emerging alongside WCs onto the Cleveland Way path. This runs along to the right to follow a fence along the edge of this open area with scattered clumps of alien conifers. Approaching denser trees the way forks: keep right on an enclosed path to a bridle-gate. Here a stone-built path climbs in the company of a wall to gain the prominent furniture on Cringle End. *This is one of those indefinable 'good places to be'. Perched on its airy promontory are a memorial topograph and seat and also an old boundary stone. Here a mild surprise awaits, for the ground continues rising further still, in dramatic fashion past the summit of Cringle Moor. Looking back Carlton Moor presents a fine shape, due in part to the old quarries on it steep north face.*

Cringle Moor is the second highest point on the North York Moors, and is a good deal shapelier than Round Hill on Urra Moor - though in step with its loftier cousin its summit mound remains largely undisturbed by the passing multitudes. The path above the dramatic plunge of its steep northern face boasts an uninterrupted view of the Cleveland Plain and the fellow Cleveland Hills. The flagged path enjoys a fine walk along the northern scarp, though all too soon the descent begins.

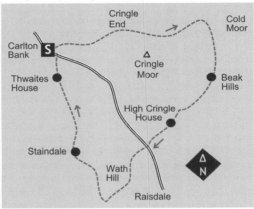

The steep descent is also rebuilt, a vast improvement on a once badly eroded and dangerous section. Passing through a few spoil heaps near the bottom, head on to a wall corner. *The spoil is from former jet mines, this once being a popular ornamental stone. Along with jet, these hills were also plundered for alum and ironstone. Evidence of the old workings abounds, good examples hereabouts being neatly arrayed along the same contour. Easily missed is a stubby old guidepost inscribed 'Kirby Road North'.* Alongside an old boundary stone in a base the path forks, bear right to a corner gate from where follow an old wall round to rise towards Cold Moor. As it starts to climb, however, abandon the Cleveland Way at a four-way guidepost and turn right across the field to a gate. A grassy track advances along the wallside, and at the end it becomes firmer and runs a part enclosed course gently down to enter the farmyard at Beak Hills.

As the driveway heads out after the last buildings, take a bridle-gate on the right with another just behind it. A path runs a few strides further to a wall-stile into a field. Descend the fenceside to a gate at the bottom, then drop diagonally down a sloping field to a gate/stile in the far corner. Maintain this pathless course across another sloping field, dropping to find a track forming in the far corner. Don't follow it however, but take a bridle-gate into the trees to cross a footbridge on a stream. A thin path slants left up the opposite bank, through bracken and trees to soon reach a stile into a field. Ascend the fenceside to a corner, where turn left to contour across the field to a fence opposite. Turn briefly right up the fenceside to soon reach a pair of stiles where you cross a tree-lined streamlet. Cross to ramshackle barns ahead, and successive stiles to their right put you onto the drive at High Cringle House. Turn right over the cattle-grid and follow the access road out onto the Carlton-Chop Gate road. *For a much easier finish turn right here.*

Cross straight over to a stile opposite and ascend the fieldside to pass beneath a stand of trees at the steeper top to reach a gate/stile. A delightful grassy track ascends the short little slope onto Wath Hill. *This diminutive knoll is a smashing viewpoint for Carlton, Cringle and Cold Moors, as well as looking down Bilsdale.* Swinging left along the crest the track angles left across to a wall-gate, but you remain on the broad top to reach an abrupt drop at the far end overlooking a vast hollow. Turn right here to slant down above the well-defined rim, a pleasant stroll that picks up another green track descending from the hill. Ignore the gate ahead at the bottom, and drop left to the very terminus of the diminishing bank: a wall-stile is found in the bottom corner alongside a fence.

Descend the rough pasture beyond, using an early gate in the fence on your left to resume down its other side. Through a gate/stile continue towards the bottom, just short of which ignore a stile in the fence into trees, and bear right to a corner stile. Now head upstream near Raisdale Beck, through several field bottoms until reaching a stile in the adjacent fence. Behind is a grassy bridge on the beck, across which ascend the field, rising right. Follow the top wall the short way to a corner gate, beyond which a good track forms as it rises gently right across rough pasture. Part way along it crosses a gate in the top wall, merging into another green way. Resume along the wallside to Staindale Farm, entering and leaving by gates. *This old farm has a fine L-shaped barn arrangement, blending neatly in with its sandstone walls and red pantile roofs.*

Follow the access road heading out, but as it quickly swings sharp right at a field corner, take a gate in front from where a grassy way advances along the hedgeside. Shortly after the next gate it passes through a gate on the left to the other side: the track ends and a thin hollowed path drops down to a gate in the wooded corner below. A steep little pull out precedes heading away with a hedge on your left again. At the end dip into a tree-lined hollow and emerge to cross a sloping pasture to a gate/stile. A grassy track now runs on to a corner gate. Resuming onwards, as the track fades and the fence turns off, keep straight on an old boundary line to a re-forming track leading to a gate at the sudden appearance of Thwaites House. Pass alongside and out along the pleasant access road back onto the road, with the finish just to the left.

Looking to Cold Moor from under Cringle Moor

INGLEBY INCLINE

A climb to the very summit of the North York Moors, and a descent along a remarkable old railway track

START *Ingleby Bank (NZ 578038; TS9 6RF)*

DISTANCE *7 miles (11^{1}4km)*

ORDNANCE SURVEY 1:25,000 MAP
Explorer OL26 - North York Moors West

ACCESS *Start from the Forestry Commission's Ingleby Greenhow car park, half a mile down a side road from the B1257 Helmsley-Stokesley road at Clay Bank Top.*
•OPEN ACCESS, first mile in plantation.

From the car park descend the road a few strides and turn right on a broad forest road. This rises a little and undulates along near the base of Greenhow Plantation, with some recently felled areas. *Ahead is your return skyline route on Greenhow Bank.* After a while the track makes a steep climb, still along the forest base, and rises to meet a harder forest road. Keep left, climbing again, before easing out to run more steadily along. *Big views look out over Greenhow Botton to Roseberry Topping's classic profile.* After the start of a brief descent, look for a gate on the left through which a bridleway comes. To your right, its continuation at once commences a steep climb through a bracken break in the pines, easing out to rise left onto a crossroads of forest tracks.

Cross straight over and the path resumes rising left, more pleasantly now to swing up to a T-junction with a level green track. Turn right for just 25 paces, and a broad path doubles back left to quickly ascend to a bridle-gate onto the open moor at Jackson's Bank. The way continues rising left, much pleasanter underfoot as it ascends though bracken into bilberry and heather. *Massive views look back over the dead flat valley bottom to Teesside, while directly across the dalehead is the very distinct line of the incline.* The ever improving path eases further on Urra Moor, and very quickly the much thinner but still clear path runs on to suddenly alight upon the Cleveland Way trade route. *By now you will be enjoying new views westwards to the Cleveland Hills switchback.*

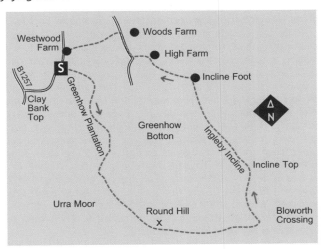

Turn left on this stone surfaced course rising gently left through the heather, soon reaching a sharp bend where it rises more steeply and stonily left, passing several boundary stones. As the way eases another track merges from the right, and the Ordnance Survey column on Round Hill appears just ahead. A little path branches left to gain it, or a little further a broader path branches off at the ancient Hand Stone. *At 1489ft/454m Round Hill is the highest point of the North York Moors, and not surprisingly*

its view is largely of rolling moorland. The name is a fitting one for this mound which is the site of a tumulus (burial cairn).

The path forges on to its gentle brow just ahead: at this point the Face Stone stands alongside. A steady descent follows, avoiding any branches until just before merging with a former railway track whose course is clearly discerned well before it is reached. *Since Round Hill the scene ahead has been one of layer upon layer of heather-clad moors, the high central ridge of the Cleveland Dome. East of Round Hill the Cleveland Hills perform a sharp dog-leg and head due north. Little else changes however, for the steep west/north scarp remains intact, with undulating moorland above and the flat plain below. Also still very much in evidence is the afforestation cloaking the steep lower slopes, seen nowhere better than on this circuit of the deep enclave of Greenhow Botton.*

While the Cleveland Way runs straight on to the railway 100 paces further, instead remain on the track as it swing left to within a minute join the railway itself. Turn left along the track-bed to pass through a cutting, emerging with big views over the whole of the walk to soon arrive at Incline Top. *The railway was built in 1861 to convey ironstone from Rosedale in the heart of the moors out to the furnaces of Teesside. The sight of trains crossing the moorland at 1300 feet would have made an inspiring sight, but the line's most fascinating feature was the incline on which cables enabled four ore-filled waggons to descend at the same time as hauling empty waggons back up onto the moor top. A climb of 770 feet was achieved within a mile at an average gradient of 1 in 5.25, and your walk takes in the full length. At the top were several employees' houses, while the old drum house was only dismantled relatively recently. Although the line closed in 1929, this is one course that won't fade into oblivion.*

Now descend the Ingleby Incline in low gear, very much a drop of two halves. The first is delightful through heather and with grassy verges, the second is through the trees. At the very bottom it merges with a forest road from the left. Continue straight on for a few minutes further to the surprisingly suburban cottages at Incline Foot. At these leave by a stile on the left, and bear right across the field to just short of the far corner. A footbridge crosses a drain to resume on the other side. *This is a good point to look back at the direct course of the incline.*

At the corner (outside a wood corner) bear right to a corner stile, becoming a nice enclosed section between drain and hedge. Alongside a concrete farm bridge at the end, keep straight on with the drain past another wood corner: High Farm House is just to the right. Entering a corner of the trees on the left, drop to a stile into a dark wooded corner to a footbridge on Ingleby Beck. A short-lived path heads downstream, quickly rising left to a wall-stile out into a field. Advance straight on to join the farm drive, which quickly runs out to join a multiple farms' access road in Ingleby Botton.

Go right a few minutes as far as the drive to Woods Farm on the right. Immediately opposite, take a gate on the left and bear slightly left across the field, aiming for Westwood Farm backed by Hasty Bank. Through a gate/stile advance along a hedgeside, and through a gate/stile at the end cross a field centre to a gate. A narrow paddock containing a pond leads on to a gate into the farm confines. Bear right outside the main cluster of buildings, then left to a gate and on through two further ones to emerge onto a road. Turn left and within minutes the road reaches the forest, and with it the end of the walk.

The Hand Stone and Round Hill, Urra Moor

THE WAINSTONES

A high-level circuit of Bilsdale's uppermost watershed, with a wealth of interest including the celebrated crags

START *Clay Bank Top (NZ 571035; TS9 7JA)*

DISTANCE *5½ miles (8¾km)*

ORDNANCE SURVEY 1:25,000 MAP
Explorer OL26 - North York Moors West

ACCESS *Start from the Forestry Commission's Clay Bank car park at Clay Bank Top on the B1257 Helmsley-Stokesley road.*

Clay Bank is the steep climb taken by the busy B1257 from the Cleveland Plain, through the pass of Clay Bank Top and down into Bilsdale. *The magnificently sited car park, virtually at the top, allows motorists to survey the plain and unmistakable Roseberry Topping from their car doors. Refreshments are often available here.* From the car park head south up the road to the very brow of the hill, and just past the lay-bys, a stone path on the left (east) rises away alongside a wall. *The route of the Cleveland Way, this splendid easy climb enjoys massive views north to the Cleveland Plain, Roseberry Topping and Teesside, and back across to the walk's second half featuring Cold Moor (overtopped by Cringle Moor) and Hasty Bank (The Wainstones hidden, for now).* A couple of bridle-gates are encountered before a steeper section precedes a gentler rise to a gate in a wall onto the heather of Urra Moor.

At this point you depart the Cleveland Way and Coast to Coast
trade route by rising just a few paces further, then turning right
along a bridleway above the wall. This commences a long course
across the moor in the company of an embankment that rapidly
forms. *Of unknown - possibly Celtic - origin, this ancient earthwork
runs for three miles in total, generally still very clearly along the
rim of the steep drop from Urra Moor to the valley.*

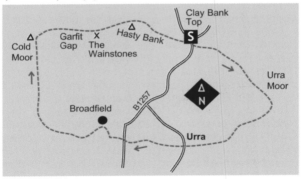

The wall drops away, and after a level stroll the path turns in
to cross a small stream. Doubling back out the delightful path
regains some of the height lost, running grandly on with the bank
to suddenly encounter a small but very pronounced nick. At this
junction of bridleways turn right down the less obvious path in a
groove to quickly arrive atop an old spoil heap. The way now drops
left through bracken to slant very gently down the moor. Joining
an old wall, the path soon reaches a bridle-gate off the moor. A
thin path descends the fieldside to emerge via a gate onto a back
lane in front of Urra House.

Turn briefly right towards Urra, but at the first bend, turn left
into the driveway of the next house. Drop to a gate on your left,
down through a brief overgrown section between old barns into an
untidy farmyard. Cross straight over the access track in front to a
stile, and descend a sloping field to the left of a sizeable pond.
Through a gate/stile descend a massive field with a tree-lined
streamlet on your left. *The Wainstones now appear silhouetted on
the west ridge of Hasty Bank's skyline.* At the very bottom corner

is a wood corner on your right: drop down the steep, grassy bank alongside to a stile in the bottom, and quickly along between streamlet and wood to a footbridge on Bilsdale Beck. A few strides further the path rises through scrub to emerge onto the B1257.

Go right just fifty paces and escape by a stile opposite. Ascend unconvincingly alongside a tree-lined streamlet on the left, a faint path culminating in scrub at the top to escape by a bridle-gate into a sheep pasture in front of Broadfield Farm. Now rise left a short way with the fence to pass through a gate in the field corner just above. Turn immediately right from this path junction, through a gap in an old wall and ascend right up the steep rough pasture to a bridle-gate in the top corner. Rise now with the old hedge-line, with bracken-covered spoil heaps just to the right. As the hedge-line swings left, rise a few paces onto a rough track. Go right a few strides to locate a slender green path up through the bracken and scrub to rapidly alight onto a stony track rising left. *If the little path was missed, advance a little further along the track above a spoil heap to then double back left up the track the path joins.*

Happily your way is straight across the stony track at a fork, on a gentler, better track slanting right through bracken. It rises to a crumbled wall to climb steeply and roughly left. Soon easing and improving, it slants across to meet another track rising by a sturdy wall. Turn right on it, rising to ease out to cross to a fence-gate ahead. Now briefly steeper, the way eases again for a gentle rise across Cold Moor's heathery flank. This grand stride quickly rises to suddenly reach a junction on Cold Moor's well-defined ridge. *Carlton Moor and Cringle Moor now appear ahead.* Your way is the most

The start from the finish: Urra Moor across Clay Bank Top

inviting, the broad path to the right along the crest of the ridge. This delectable, undulating stroll with super views leads unfailingly all the way along to the summit, at the moor's northernmost point.

Arrival on a popular highway at Cold Moor's bare summit is emphasized by the stone-built path: this will remain underfoot for the greater part of the return to Clay Bank Top. Turn right to begin a rapid descent to Garfit Gap, passing through spoil heaps from old jet mines: ahead, the Wainstones arouse anticipation. Through a gate at the bottom the briefly grassy path dips through two fields before the very short re-ascent to the rock pinnacles.

The Wainstones are Hasty Bank's pride and joy, a tumbled group of crags and boulders popular with rock climbers. The path picks an easy way between the boulders before crossing Hasty Bank's lengthy top. *Though not the highest point on the Cleveland ridge, this is arguably the finest. The splendid path clings to its northern edge, as the flat Cleveland Plain contrasts sharply with Bilsdale stretching away south.* Towards the end the adjacent cliffs are of a serious scale, emphasized by an unbroken fall from just off the path. The descent is again steep, beginning at the end of the cliffs and dropping through a few spoil heaps to join a forestry track at a kissing-gate. Instead of following the track the path continues down by the wall to emerge back onto the road at Clay Bank Top.

At the Wainstones

BILSDALE WEST MOOR

*An initial steep pull and quiet fieldpaths sandwich
a superb walk along high moorland tracks*

START *Chop Gate (SE 559993; TS9 7JN)*

DISTANCE *5³⁄4 miles (9¹⁄4km)*

ORDNANCE SURVEY 1:25,000 MAP
Explorer OL26 - North York Moors West

ACCESS *Start from the village centre, car park by village hall.*

Chop Gate (pronounced 'Yat') is, even with the support of
attractive neighbour Seave Green, a small settlement, but is still
a focal point in lonely Bilsdale. A major function is as a meeting
point for some of the challenge walks that pass this way. The tiny
Wesleyan chapel of 1858 is almost hidden at the road junction,
while a war memorial stands opposite. A tablet on the school
informs that it was erected by the Earl of Feversham in 1909. Next
door is the old school house, while a little further is the Buck Inn
(with tearoom), one of only two pubs in Bilsdale. Between the two
is the old smithy, bearing a lintel inscribed '1826 WR'. Raisdale and
Bilsdale Becks merge to form the River Seph by the car park.

Leave the car park not by the entrance, but by an enclosed
track crossing a bridge at the opposite end, near the WCs. Through
a gate/stile it starts the steep climb up Trennet. Almost at once,
at the first bend right, a green footpath branches off it to ascend

directly through gorse then bracken, in sunken fashion. Rising to be level with a bridle-gate by the boundary on your left, don't pass through but stay on the path veering right uphill, to quickly emerge into a large open pasture. A thin path continues up alongside the bracken to a gate in a fence above: the true right of way takes a stile to your left on the line of the still sunken way. *Bilsdale mast rises over to the left, while Hasty Bank and Chop Gate look good.*

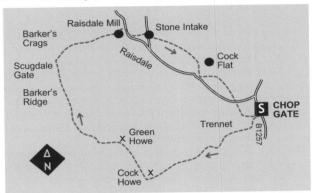

The path rises again to a line of grassy spoil heaps, veering left beneath them to merge with a direct path from the stile. The way rises left to a stile in a fence, then slants much more gently left up to a gate/stile in a wall onto open moorland. Immediately crossing a reedy bridleway, the path resumes slanting up through bracken, quickly easing out into heather. Meeting a fence from the left, it then runs on by a wall to the start of an unexpected high-level plantation. Part way along, veer right on the narrowing path for fifty strides to join a much clearer path. *The view over much of Bilsdale culminates in a fine Cleveland Hills skyline to the north, featuring Carlton Moor, Cringle Moor, Cold Moor and Hasty Bank.*

This excellent path runs on at length from the trees, and as the plantation turns off, your super path continues its gentle rise through grouse butts to the prominent Cock Howe on the moor top. *Now on the main ridge, you have earned views west to Black Hambleton and beyond to the Yorkshire Dales. Both Cock Howe and forthcoming Green Howe are well-defined mounds, and like countless others on the moors are likely to be the burial sites of ancient chieftains. On a more modern note, the tall TV mast is just a mile and a half south of Cock Howe on the ridge.*

From Cock Howe a broader way runs for less than 100 strides to meet a shooters' track along the crest of the broad ridge. This is now followed right to the walk's summit at around 1325ft/404m on Green Howe. *Along here is a sudden revelation of the industry of Teesside between Carlton and Cringle Moors.* Dropping very gently left from Green Howe another track is joined at a T-junction. Turn right here to decline steadily down Barker's Ridge. *With such easy walking savour to the full the magnificent panorama from this broad ridge: the return route through Raisdale is down to the right. A pleasant surprise comes when the improbable profile of Roseberry Topping slots into the Cringle Moor-Cold Moor gap, while another sudden appearance is that of Scugdale down to the left. Ahead is the mile-long line of Barker's Crags fronting Carlton Moor beyond Scugdale Gate, and the unmistakable contour-perfect piles of spoil from former jet mines.*

The track swings right to drop to a gate in an intervening fence at Scugdale Gate. Just a little further is a junction where one branch rises left to a fence fronting the now very close Barker's Crags: here bear right on a steady decline towards a gate where the track leaves the moor. Your way, however, clings to moorland a little longer on the bridle-path remaining outside the wall. It descends, crossing a forestry access track en route to drop to a gate in a reedy corner. Pass through and descend this old way (Mill Lane), a largely pleasant old holloway passing through further gates as it drops to emerge onto an access road alongside Raisdale Mill. Turn left on this through the assorted attractive buildings, quickly swinging right up onto the road through Raisdale.

Turning right, you could opt to follow this quiet back road all the way back to Chop Gate. However, easy variations add interest. Rising away from the trees as it swings right, take a bridle-gate on the left and ascend the field with a wall to your right. Through a gate near the top continue up to a stile at the top onto a narrow access road. Go briefly right until immediately after the nice grouping at Stone Intake Farm. As the road starts to drop away, take an access road through a gate on the left, rising and swinging right to a farm at High West Cote.

Immediately before its yard take a gate on the right and go left along the field top to a corner stile. Resume along a field top beneath gorse and scrub to a gate at the end, then rise slightly across a sloping field centre to a ladder-stile in the opposite wall. Entering dense bracken, remain with the fence on your right, a thin but easy path running along the bracken base to the fence corner. As it drops away, advance straight on a grassy path still through bracken, but opening out into grassy patches. After only sixty paces make use of a grassy patch to drop right, possibly locating a thin trod down through bracken to almost instantly escape at a stile in a fence below. Drop down the sloping pasture to a gate where the Cock Flat farm road joins the valley road.

Either simply remain on this for a few minutes, or take a stile alongside the farm gate. Head away with the fence to your left to a corner gate sharing its latch-hook with the next gate. From this slant right down the field to a farm bridge on a tree-lined stream. Through the gate behind bear right to trace the stream, keeping your distance for the first stile then on above reeds to a gate, then on again to a stile back out onto the road. Cross straight over to another, and trace the stream down to its entry into Raisdale Beck. Now accompany the main beck downstream, over an intervening stile and along a final fieldside to a stile back into the car park.

At Raisdale Mill

TRIPSDALE

Varied walking in a hidden offshoot of Bilsdale

START *Bilsdale (SE 572961; TS9 7LB)*

DISTANCE *5³4 miles (9¹4km)*

ORDNANCE SURVEY 1:25,000 MAP
Explorer OL26 - North York Moors West

ACCESS *Start from a sizeable lay-by at the entrance to The Grange, on the west side of the B1257 2¹2 miles south of Chop Gate. •OPEN ACCESS - see page 8. Probably best avoided after wet spells and in late summer due to a section of the path in the heart of Tripsdale being plagued by over-zealous bracken.*

Head south along the road over the bridge on Ledge Beck, and turn left at the first opportunity up a driveway serving a host of farms. Almost at once turn left off this along another drive, and remain on it until it turns sharp right. Here take a kissing-gate on the left and cross the field to a footbridge on the beck into Hill End Wood. *Hard by the bridge a tiny iron-rich spring gurgles, while in springtime the wood has a carpet of bluebells.* A slender path heads briefly upstream, but after crossing a streamlet it slants up the steep wooded bank, easing higher up to run to a ladder-stile at the top. Head up the hedgeside, bearing left at the top to a bridle-gate onto a farm drive. Go right the short way up to Hill End Farm.

Turn right opposite the house, and on through a paddock to the end. From a stile on the left a path ascends a scrubby enclosure to a stile in a gateway at the top, entering a bracken-filled pasture. Advance a few strides, crossing straight over a thin path and rising just a few unkempt strides onto a grassy path coming from a gate over to the left. Turn right on this as it contours along to join and follow a wall. *Hidden Tripsdale is slowly revealed ahead now, its outstanding scenery featuring some lovely woodland.*

The path now runs on into denser bracken as it reaches a stile at the foot of a descending wall. The bracken will dominate until beyond the beck crossing ahead. An enclosed spell soon opens out again, and during this near-level stage several old cross-walls are met. Reaching a wall with a tiny enclosure to the right, the true descent to the beck begins. The path is initially a little thinner but still very evident as it slants down towards Tripsdale Beck, emerging at a heathery tract just short of a gate at the foot of the final wall.

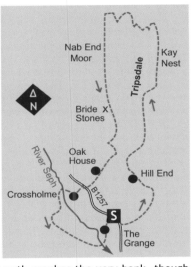

Just beyond the gate the path reaches the very bank, though a land-slipped tree has obscured the natural crossing point here. Dropping down the rougher bank and crossing on scattered stones, head upstream only fifty strides to escape a mossy tract, and you will encounter the original route slanting up from the stream in sunken fashion. Rather moist and reedy, within 100 strides it slants right up to an old gateway. The old way climbs directly away from here, still reedy and abandoned but persevere and it will improve to emerge onto a level grass path. Go left on this much more appealing way which quickly starts to slant up at an easy angle. As bracken slowly gives way to heather, the views also open out more.

The path passes above a solitary tree and onto a grassy alp: no more than thirty strides further, as the path enters a minor sunken section, take a grassy trod contouring left. This rises very slightly to almost immediately gain the crest of Kay Nest, a superb section as a thin path runs along its length. Though not always well seen, at one stage this becomes a cliff of reasonable proportions. *If you missed the trod, the sunken path quickly fades and levels out on the open moor: simply bear left for a minute to the obvious edge where you will pick up the direct route.*

Beyond the end of the edge a bulldozed shooters' track is joined, and steep zigzags work down to the beck. Across, the track begins an immediate, steep re-ascent. *Fine views look right to Tripsdale's lonely upper reaches.* The climb soon eases to undertake a big slant left, then doubles back right and quickly sharp left again to climb to the brow. *The view ahead embraces Bilsdale West Moor, Carlton Moor, Cringle Moor, Cold Moor and the Wainstones on Hasty Bank, with Chop Gate and Raisdale below.*

A T-junction is reached just short of a prominent boundary stone with a wall just behind. Take the inviting branch left, an improving track that runs through heather along the near-level crest of the ridge of Nab End Moor. In a little less than a mile this will take you unfailingly to a tall, beckoning cairn on Nab Ridge. *This massive cairn is an obvious halting place, with great valley views as Tripsdale runs to your left, with Bilsdale straight ahead. Immediately beneath it are the Bride Stones, an ancient circular enclosure of upright stones.* Remain on the track which narrows before reaching a bridle-gate at converging walls. Through it a green wallside path continues through bracken, along a wallside towards the top corner of a plantation.

Just before reaching the trees the path swings right for a big curve down through the bracken, doubling back to a gateway into the forest. A path cuts through the corner of it to emerge through a fence gap at the bottom. In an area of new tree planting, go briefly left to the start of a sunken way. Drop down this also briefly: quickly opening out, go right on the start of a different sunken way, slanting down beneath undergrowth and new plantings to a hairpin bend in front of a gate in a wall. The path then drops left, down above the wall to a gate at the bottom by old sheep pens. From the gate behind, with Oak House just below, bear left across the field top to a footbridge on a stream. Turn down the other side to a stile below, and down outside the house to another stile. This sends an enclosed way down with the stream, and in the bottom cross a stile to resume down through a few trees. Emerging at a stile continue down again, pleasantly enclosed. Through a gate at the bottom the stream is crossed and a fieldside leads down by the stream to a gate onto the B1257.

Go right a few paces and head down the short drive opposite to Crossholme Farm. Immediately after the farmhouse turn right through the colourful yard, keeping on at the end as a continuing drive runs out to bridge the River Seph and doubles back across a field. As it slants uphill to double back to the house at Beacon Guest just above, rise left a few steps and turn left along a little grass path running to a gate just ahead. Through it the continuing path enjoys a lovely stroll along a fenceside beneath a steep bracken bank. At the end take the left-hand of two gates to run a briefly enclosed section to Stable Holme Farm. Just past the buildings its driveway joins a surfaced access road. Go left, bridging the Seph again and rising through the houses at The Grange to re-emerge onto the road alongside the lay-by.

The Bride Stones

ROPPA EDGE

A very straightforward walk utilising two parallel tracks: extensive Bilsdale views, few gradients, easy navigation

START *Newgate Bank (SE 564889; YO62 5LT)*

DISTANCE *5$\frac{3}{4}$ miles (9$\frac{1}{4}$km)*

ORDNANCE SURVEY 1:25,000 MAP
Explorer OL26 - North York Moors West

ACCESS *Start from the Forestry Commission car park at top of Newgate Bank, on B1257 five miles north of Helmsley.*

Roppa Edge is not named on the OS map, but is known variously as Ayton, Rievaulx and Helmsley Banks. Newgate Bank is a well-known hill which the Stokesley-Helmsley road surmounts to leave Bilsdale for the moor edge run down into Helmsley. Without even leaving the car park with its intimate parking bays, spectacular views can be enjoyed. From the main car park return almost to the road, then take a wide forestry track on the left heading directly away from the road. After merging with a track from the right, bear left on a nicer track to quickly emerge from the forest.

Here it begins an endlessly gentle rise over the heathery sweep of Rievaulx Moor, with much silver birch lining the conifer blocks to your left. *Views over the trees constantly improve as Bilsdale leads the eye to the classic Cleveland skyline of Cringle Moor, Cold Moor and Hasty Bank. Certainly, as Bilsdale gives way to the moors to its east, to Bransdale and Rudland Rigg, it engenders little doubt that the North York Moors is the greatest expanse of heather moor in England. Here you are on a classic example of the Tabular Hills layout, this outward leg running along the top of its northward plunge: the conifers are also a typical feature, though as height is gained there is more heather than conifer alongside you.*

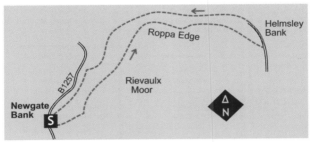

Eventually the track arrives at the Ordnance Survey column at 1076ft/328m atop Roppa Edge. *From the top almost all of the western moors are visible, and to the right neighbouring Birk Nab looks impressive.* Just a few minutes' dead-level walk along the broad ridge beyond the trig point leads along to a narrow road at a parking area above Helmsley Bank. Double back left down to the road's demise at a crossroads of forest tracks. Head along the track to the left, which soon escapes confinement to run along the wooded base of Roppa Edge with big moorland sweeps to the right. Little changes for a long time as the track keeps losing a little height. *Easterside Hill appears ahead with the spurs of Black Hambleton beyond.* Ultimately the plantations return as the track proceeds to lose more height.

Exactly as the B1257 up Newgate Bank appears ahead, a guide-post sends a bridle-path left: it climbs briefly steeply then quickly swings right for a sustained, uniform slant up through the trees. At the top it levels out abruptly and runs a level course along to the right, only path-width amid nice open surrounds. Before long it arrives beneath the observation platform at the car park: a tiny path cuts back up to it. *From here Ryedale and Bilsdale fan out towards the high moors: unseen just below you they merge at Seph Mouth.* The car park, meanwhile, is in the trees directly behind.